IT'S THEIR BUSINESS, TOO
A Manager's Guide to Employee Awareness

Daniel Dickinson

AMA Management Briefing

AMA MEMBERSHIP PUBLICATIONS DIVISION
AMERICAN MANAGEMENT ASSOCIATION

Library of Congress Cataloging in Publication Data

Dickinson, Daniel, 1950-
  It's their business, too.

  (AMA management briefing)
  Bibliography: p.
  1. Employees, Training of. 2. Economics—Study and teaching. I. Title. II. Title: Employee Awareness.
  III. Series.
  HF5549.5.T7D48   1985   658.3′124   85-1226
  ISBN 0-8144-2313-2

©1985 AMA Membership Publications Division

American Management Association, New York.
All rights reserved. Printed in the United States of America.

This Management Briefing has been distributed to all members enrolled in the American Management Association. Copies may be purchased at the following single-copy rates: AMA members, $7.50. Nonmembers, $10.00. Students, $3.75 (upon presentation of a college/university identification card at an AMA bookstore). Faculty members may purchase 25 or more copies for classroom use at the student discount rate (order on college letterhead).

This publication may not be reproduced, stored in a retrieval system, or transmitted in whole or in part, in any form or by any means, electronic, mechanical, photocopying, recording, or otherwise, without the prior written permission of AMA Membership Publications Division, 135 West 50th Street, New York, N.Y. 10020.

First Printing

About the Author

Dan Dickinson is president of the Productivity Communication Center (PCC), a Boston-based foundation that assists corporations in developing and managing employee programs.

Prior to joining PCC, Dickinson was active in the fields of business, public affairs, and education. As counsel to the New York Senate Higher Education committee, he wrote (and saw enacted) legislation on open government, student assistance, and business-education cooperation. As the regional director of a national lobbying organization, he traveled extensively in the northeast, encouraging citizens to become involved in the legislative process.

In 1979, Dickinson became president of the newly formed Productivity Communication Center. In that role he has designed awareness programs for over 60 corporations, provided management training in employee awareness for 200 more, and run over 600 awareness sessions for rank-and-file employees in firms throughout the United States. Mr. Dickinson has worked with General Motors, Hallmark, Huffy, Cabot Corporation, Norton, Folger's Division of Procter and Gamble, Dennison, and John Hancock Insurance.

Mr. Dickinson has spoken on employee involvement throughout

the United States and in Canada, and has written articles on business issues for such publications as *Industry Week, National Review, Ohio Business,* and *Commonweal.*

Acknowledgments

Whoever said that "there's no such thing as a free lunch" was a fool. Who we are and what we accomplish result, in large part, from the greatest free lunch in history: the heritage of the past, the inspiration of our peers, and the solace, support, and perseverance of our friends and families.

Among the many people who assisted in preparing this study were Ray Shamie, chairman of Metal Bellows and founder of PCC; Ron Graham and Sarah Kelly, who've kept the torch aloft at Ray's company; Charles Orem, president of Bird-Johnson Company, who suggested the project to the AMA; AMA's Don Bohl, who patiently waited for it; Ruth Conroy, who helped develop the ideas; Charles Wolfe and Diana Clark Grafmuller, for background on Fred Clark and AEF; and my associates at PCC, Brenda Bronson, Tony Faunce, Jean Flanagan, and Tom Moccia, whose contributions have been innumerable.

Special thanks go to my wife Kelley, who urged, sympathized, prodded, and kept pouring coffee (which she hates), until I got it done.

Contents

1 An Idea Whose Time Has Returned   9
2 The Economic Crisis: A Decade of Dislocations   14
3 Who Are Today's Employees?   18
4 The First Experiments   36
5 Modern Employee Awareness   47
6 Getting Started   57
7 Managing Awareness   67
8 Afterword: The Greatest Revolution   75
Appendix A   77
Appendix B   85
References   87

1

An Idea Whose Time Has Returned

On December 5, 1933, Fred G. Clark and his friends did something they hadn't done, at least legally, for 14 years. They took a drink.

A prominent Cleveland oil executive still in his 30s, Clark had been a leader of the movement to repeal prohibition. Successful in his crusade, he looked around on that December morning for new worlds to conquer.

Clark found his cause in the nation's ever-deepening economic depression. The fact of the matter was that by the time liquor again became legal in America there was precious little to celebrate about. By late 1933, over 10 million Americans, nearly 25 percent of the workforce, had lost their jobs in the collapse. Banks were failing, soup lines were forming, despair was everywhere. Labor strife had increased dramatically, too: between 1925 and 1935, the annual number of strikes had tripled. With increasing frequency, industrial conflicts degenerated into violent melees, as commentator after commentator alleged that capitalism, at least as America had known it, was finished. By the late 1930s, nearly a third of the population had decided that socialism in America was inevitable. Interestingly, more businessmen agreed with this proposition than did workers.[1]

Concerned that high rates of unemployment, widespread plant shutdowns, and the concurrent economic hardship could lead, in America as it had in Europe, to the spread of radical ideologies, and deeply worried about the nation's ability to remain productive in the face of rising unionism and hostile attitudes toward business, Clark felt that America could simply no longer afford to remain a nation of economic illiterates. Further, he believed that the détente between management and labor was crucial to ending the perpetual strife that was draining the vitality of American industry.

In 1939, Clark, along with Cleveland ad executive Richard Rimanoczy and a group of like-minded business economists, founded the American Economic Foundation. The goal of the organization was to communicate with American workers the facts—as AEF saw them—about business, the marketplace, and their companys' bottom lines. Agreeing with Peter Drucker that "there is no greater danger to a free economy than the hostility of employees toward profit,"[2] Clark focused much atten-

Drawing by Lorenz; © 1970
The New Yorker Magazine, Inc.

"And though in 1969, as in previous years, your company had to contend with spiralling labor costs, exorbitant interest rates, and unconscionable government interference, management was able once more, through a combination of deceptive marketing practices, false advertising, and price fixing, to show a profit which, in all modesty, can only be called excessive."

tion on incentives. Deciding that "profit is the cost of using the tools of production,"[3] AEF counseled workers to consider profits a "rent on tools." Clark was equally concerned with giving employees a better understanding of their businesses. Long before it became popular (and it still hasn't caught on in some quarters), he advocated that companies show workers their bottom lines, and that they "simplify" their annual statements to make them comprehensible to nonaccountants. Further, Clark wanted everyone to understand that, ultimately, "the customer is the person who provides employment and payroll."[4] Altogether, it was hoped that when Americans understood the system and where they and their firms fit in, they'd not only be better educated workers, they'd also be more motivated ones. Employee awareness was born.

FALSE OPTIMISM AND THE DECLINE OF AWARENESS

For a quarter of a century, Clark and like-minded contemporaries preached this gospel and, despite opposition, made some inroads. Although the unions, often all-too-accurately, viewed the early programs as antilabor, and although many employees saw the economics offerings as "too theoretical," the concept spread. By the late fifties, thousands of firms had run "poster and payroll-stuffer" economics programs. A number of the more venturesome actually hosted face-to-face programs for the rank and file—a daring concept in the postwar years. General Electric, an early enthusiast, went so far as to hire a prominent actor with a persuasive union background to serve as spokesman for its economic education efforts. As recently as his 1976 presidential run, Ronald Reagan was still bringing audiences to their feet with his celebrated "green index card" economics stem-winder, originally delivered in the fifties to GE employees and business executives.

There is, of course, no way of fully knowing how many people were reached through these efforts, or what effect, if any, they had on "economic illiteracy." Still, Clark's own early sixties estimate that 2,000 corporations and three and one half million employees had participated at one point or another was probably not wildly off the mark. Economic awareness had arrived. Or had it?

As America's prosperity boomed in the Eisenhower years, the

It's Their Business, Too—11

employee programs faded, as did, incidently, the then-nascent quality circles movement. At the beginning of the fifties, hundreds of major American corporations had initiated significant awareness efforts and were making headway in the field. But by the time Jack Kennedy reached the White House, the companies making substantive contributions to awareness probably numbered fewer than a dozen. What had happened?

The reason most generally given for the demise of employee awareness in the mid-fifties and sixties is that the programs had lost touch with the times. Observers with increasing frequency derided the efforts as "propaganda" and felt that the strident tone of much of what had been produced during the cold war years was simply out of "synch" in the sixties—a time when the ethos was "mellow yellow," everything was "relative," and the climate was "cool." In an era of seemingly limitless opportunity, at the verge of the "space age," did we really need pamphlets explaining why, to give a particularly lurid example, "Communists Hate Christ"?

Criticized too was the effectiveness of the programs. So what if people have a better understanding of economics? How does that make them more productive? Were we really reaching people? Or were we simply hitting them with information they didn't really want? Program content fell under scrutiny. Was profit, after all, just "rent for tools"? During my first year of running awareness programs, the validity of this last objection was brought home in a singular way. After an employee session, a grizzled machinist lumbered up and asked whether I was

---

At base, the reason employee awareness was allowed to die on the vine was simply that businesses perceived that it was no longer needed. Everything was going just fine, thank you. As a popular expression put it: "If it ain't broke, don't fix it."

---

aware that they used to do what I was doing—explaining economics to workers—back in the fifties? I said I'd heard that. How, I wondered, had he liked the programs back then? He was always happy to be informed, he told me, but he hadn't really liked the "message." So far as he could tell, the point was that the machines did it all, and that the individual didn't count for much. If this was the "message" that was coming across, it was exactly the opposite of the theme that a good employee program should convey.

At the bottom line, though, the decline of employee awareness had little to do with these issues. As far as the materials being "out of step," it would have been easy enough for corporations to update them, had the desire been there. Regarding ineffectiveness, that too could have been resolved had companies wished to labor over the issue: problem solving, after all, is what corporate management is supposed to be all about. At base, the reason employee awareness was allowed to die on the vine was simply that businesses perceived that it was no longer needed. Everything was going just fine, thank you. As a popular expression put it: "If it ain't broke, don't fix it."

In 1958, as America entered a boom of prosperity, John Kenneth Galbraith published *The Affluent Society*. In the book the liberal economist declares that "the problem of production has been solved."[5] Henceforth, Galbraith seemed to say, America's corporations would experience continual growth. And although corporate executives bridled at Galbraith's calls for more regulation and government control of business, they implicitly accepted his notion of their own infallibility.

For a long time, Galbraith's predictions held true. The fifties boom translated, during the sixties, into our greatest period of sustained growth. We seemed to have the Midas touch: everything we put a finger on turned to gold. Thus, why talk about profits when there was plenty of money to go around? And why bother people about understanding business? The system was working, after all. Lastly, it would be nice if people knew about productivity, but the unions get mad when you mention it, so why rock the boat? If we run into a problem, we can always buy a new machine.

"Everything may be endured," Goethe wrote, "but continual prosperity." In the 1960s we got fat, happy, and complacent. Somehow, we slipped our moorings; we floated far from the basics of what makes a business or an economy succeed. The ballast of America's economic greatness began to list. When the storm struck, we hardly knew what hit us.

2

The Economic Crisis: A Decade of Dislocations

In his cautionary 1970 international bestseller *The American Challenge*, the prominent French journalist Jean Jacques Servan-Schreiber worried about the danger posed by American world economic dominance. The author sounded a warning note: U.S. businesses would achieve mastery "not because of their money resources or technology but because of their corporate organizational ability."[6] Ten years later, in their equally strident attack on corporate ineptitude, economists Bennet Harrison and Barry Bluestone used *The Deindustrialization of America* to argue that our nation's collapse as a industrial power was imminent unless radical surgery was performed on our economic and political structures.[7] In a very real sense, these two volumes could serve as bookends to a decade of dislocations.

The insidious approach of serious economic hardships that began to surface in the seventies should have been predictable. Despite the pervasive prosperity, productivity had begun its long decline fairly early in the game. By the late sixties, the slowdown in the rate of growth was well under way. The savings rate, inhibited by the gradual increase in inflation and the dramatic rise in the total level of taxation, began to decline, too. Suddenly it became more difficult to spur production rates through capital investments. At the same time employee attitudes began to shift ominously during the sixties: as early as 1966 confidence in business began its long and painful collapse while workplace dissatisfaction—in a time of unparalleled wage and benefits growth—grew unaccountably. Meanwhile, out in the streets, social change triggered a backlash against corporations. Executives were suddenly blamed for racism, poverty, environmental problems, and the Vietnam war. Bob Dylan rasped a sinister warning, voicing the collective cry of the counterculture: "You'd better take care of business, Mr. Businessman."

By the early 1970s, the effects of public dissatisfaction and social unrest were breaking through into the workplace. In *Working,* his 1972 classic, journalist Studs Terkel interviewed hundreds of American employees, asking them to describe their jobs. The picture that emerged from the volume was one of almost unrelieved discontent, nowhere more so than in the auto industry. There Jim Grayson, a spot welder, told Terkel that "whenever we make a mistake, we always say, 'Don't worry about it. Some dingaling will buy it'."[8] Such attitudes, later in the decade, would translate into excessive warranty costs. By 1980, 64 percent of the owners of American cars were reporting mechanical difficulties in the first six months, as opposed to 35 percent American owners of Japanese cars. Grayson's neighbor "on the line," welder Phil Stallings, was similarly distraught. He asked, "What price do they put on me? Look at the price they put on the machine. If that machine breaks down, there's someone out there to fix it . . . If I break down, I'm just pushed to the other side. . . ."[9] Such feelings, later on, helped generate the startling drop in productivity experienced in the late seventies. Meanwhile, their supervisor, foreman Wheeler Stanley, acknowledged that some people weren't happy with the way things were going. "The boss ain't always right," he declared, "but he's the boss."[10] This insistence on managerial suzerainty in the face of increasing evidence of inferior managerial performance likewise made its contribution to the collapse.

When the difficulties appeared, they arrived with alarming suddenness. The 1970 recession merged into the oil crisis of 1973, which in turn ran into the 1974 recession. With the election of Jimmy Carter came a brief return to prosperity followed by double-digit inflation, soaring interest rates, high unemployment, and, in 1980, yet another recession.

Our ability to run our businesses at significantly lower energy costs than other nations was killed by OPEC; our lead in capital investment was destroyed by inflation and soaring tax bills; our vaunted expertise in people management was shown to be lacking by the unrelenting descent of both efficiency improvement rates and job satisfaction. One by one, we were quickly losing those advantages which had earned us center stage in the economic theater. As the decade progressed, it became increasingly clear that these were strong contenders for the leading role waiting in the wings.

The strongest challenge came from Japan. Throughout the seventies, the nation's productivity improvements far excelled our own, while it posted savings rates three times ours. As a result, in field after field, American products were driven off world markets by Japanese goods, at first because they were cheaper, and then because they were both cheaper and better. Industrialized states like West Germany, France, and even Italy were making similar if less spectacular gains. Worse, some of the "N.D.Cs." (newly developing countries) entered the competitive lists after emerging from the long postimperialist slumber common to new socialist states. Taiwan, Hong Kong, Singapore, and Korea became low-wage, high-output industrial meccas. And as their products flooded American markets, jobs were lost. All told, we were suffering, economically speaking, from what MIT economist Lester Thurow called "death by a thousand cuts."[11]

In 1980, the collapse began in earnest. The steel industry, that mighty girder of the American economy, suffered a near-crushing retrenchment. It was hardly unexpected; productivity in the industry had held an unremitting straight line for 17 years. Even so, the human cost of the decline was disastrous. Autos suffered a similar crisis, as did rubber, machine tools, and a dozen others. Unemployment spiraled to levels unseen since Depression years, factories closed or operated at minimum capacity, and bankruptcies proliferated. Meanwhile, public attitudes toward the business community, already low, sunk to new depths. By 1982, only 13 percent of Americans were telling pollsters they had confidence in business while over 50 percent of the people were describing executives as "generally immoral and unethical." At a time when corporate profitability was sinking to record lows, people by vast majorities were stating that they considered profits too high and exhorting that they be brought down to more reasonable limits.

The irony in all this was that if the problems of the seventies had proved one thing, it was that people were more important now than ever before. In an era in which technologies were becoming the same for all the leading players, in a time in which world markets in capital, resources, and energy had equalized traditional discrepancies between competitors and nations, the difference between success and failure for both economies and firms would lie increasingly in the commitment and willingness of the individual employee to innovate. We were failing at people management—once one of our strongest talents—at precisely the point at which those skills had reached their apogee of importance.

In 1944 Fred Clark had warned that "the problem is people." On that score, at least, Clark got it dead wrong. People weren't the problem, they were the solution. But how did you get them to realize it? For that matter, how did you get management to understand? Even more basically, just who are the people?

3

Who Are Today's Employees?

Industry, trade, and all other branches of the economy rise and fall with the personal influence of individual talents. And this freedom is endangered as much by corporations as by governments. Both replace the free will of the creative individual with a plan. Both inhibit the rise of those who are capable, because it is more convenient to work with mediocrity.
—Oswald Spengler, *Newbau Des Deutschen Reiches* (1924)

In 1924, when Spengler wrote those words, Taylorism, or "scientific management," was the rage in industries in both Europe and America. By standardizing, analyzing, and planning the processes of work, many believed that businesses could enjoy higher productivity and profits while workers would receive better pay and benefits. Taylorism was advertised as the perfect win-win. While it would not be for another 40 some years that Galbraith would declare that the production problem had been solved, it was confidently believed from the early years of this century that the key to the riddle, at least, had been found.

Even so, "scientific management" had its critics right from the start. Moreover, it had some rather dubious admirers. While rejecting virtually every other manifestation of capitalism, Lenin had embraced Taylorism with the passion of a true enthusiast. To this day, the bulk of Soviet industry is organized along "scientific" principles that have nothing to do with Marxism, without notably dramatic results.

Probably the most prominent of the objectors was Harvard's Elton Mayo, who, commenting on the tendency of "scientific management" to dehumanize the workplace, declared that "no social system can be considered satisfactory which deprives the great majority of mankind of every vestige of autonomy."[12] During the Hawthorne experiments of the twenties and thirties, which Mayo supervised with colleague Chester Barnard, the pair demonstrated that "attention to employees, not work conditions per se, has the dominant effect on productivity."[13] In short, people rather than processes produce gains. On approaches to the workforce, the ideas of Taylor, Mayo, and Barnard have framed the debate ever since. Discussions concerning such concepts as Theories X, Y, and Z or those involving "job enhancement" are in truth variations on these two basic themes.

Early employee awareness programs were based on an essentially Taylor-oriented world view. They presumed that employees were rational, self-interested, and motivated by money and security concerns. The employee addressed by Fred Clark was the "economic man." He was the guy that Samuel Gompers, founder of the AFL, said wanted "more." By contrast, some of management's newer programs, such as quality circles, seem very near to the Mayo point of view. These programs presume that employees will be self-motivated toward efficiency if interest is shown and they're given some ideas about what to do. Which approach most truly reaches today's employees? What role can employee awareness play in supplying motivation?

TODAY'S EMPLOYEE: A PARADOX

At the time Taylor was doing his research, determining the attitudes of workers was largely a matter of guesswork. By Elton Mayo's day, the survey industry had entered its infancy. Through the pioneering work of Gallup, Roper, and others, those interested in understanding the employee had at least a measure of facts to supplement their opinions, observations, and suppositions.

In today's world, by contrast, we're deluged with data on employees. The major national survey firms routinuely scan the general public; business "think tanks" provide the same services for industry; and most major corporations periodically poll their own people to gauge employee sentiment. Out of this enormous collection of readings certain patterns have begun to take shape, patterns that warrant serious study by any corporate executive who hopes to create a program that will truly reach today's employee.

The portrait of today's employees according to these readings is dominated by splashes of contrasting colors. On the one hand, they're vociferous defenders of "free enterprise"—while on the other, their hostility to profits is undisguised. They want to work—but increasingly dislike their jobs. They're for quality—but often don't believe they are producing it.

Probably the most comprehensive selection of survey research on public and employee attitudes is a compilation of materials put together by the U.S. Chamber of Commerce in 1981 entitled *Public Attitudes Toward Business and the Enterprise System*. Although never released to the public, the study served as the source for a series of monographs published by the Chamber in 1982 concerning worker and public attitudes on a variety of topics. Using many of the same surveys presented in the Chamber volume, as well as others not covered, social scientists William Schneider and Seymour Martin Lipset attempted in *The Confidence Gap* (1983) to analyze not just how workers felt about business, but how Americans as a whole were reacting to all forms of institutional leadership in the eighties. Between these two texts, we have a mass of data regarding who today's employees are.

The portrait of today's employees according to these readings is dominated by splashes of contrasting colors. On the one hand, they're vociferous defenders of "free enterprise"—while on the other, their hostility to profits is undisguised. They want to work—but increasingly dislike their jobs. They're for quality—but often don't believe they are producing it. Probably most important, although they're passionate believers in "freedom" and the "American way"—they are, as individuals, deeply alienated and generally distrustful of those who have power over them. Today's employee is a paradox.

How do employees view the world? We'll review some specific areas and draw some general conclusions.

PROFIT: WHAT'S THAT GOT TO DO WITH ME?

"Profitability," Peter Drucker once wrote, "is the sovereign criterion of the enterprise." It's a concept—and a phrase—familiar to every business school graduate. Even so, a realization of what profit is all about—even after 30 years of "economic education," Mobil ads, and exhortations by corporate executives—has still failed to register with the average American. According to any number of polls, the public thinks that the average profit on the sales dollar after taxes is somewhere between 25 percent to 40 percent. Sindlinger, in 1979, informed us that 61 percent of the people feel that profits are "too high," while in 1981 48 percent of the public told the U.S. Chamber Research Center that business firms make "unreasonable profits." Fifty percent of the citizenry told Yankelovich (1979) that "big business is overly concerned with profits at the expense of good products and good service."

Interestingly, people's views of the profitability of particular industries reflect their own attitudes toward that business: but in a negative way. The auto industry, which is generally not liked, is seen as highly profitable. In 1981, not a banner year for the Big Three, the public estimated their profits at 41 percent (they actually lost money). By contrast, the airlines are usually seen by the public as poor financial performers, although historically they've been among the most profitable. Airlines are probably the most highly regarded business by the public.

PRODUCTIVITY: JUST GIVE ME A CHANCE, I'LL SHOW THEM HOW

Imagine you're a salesman. At the conclusion of your presentation, your potential customer (a) doesn't know what the product is, (b)

Exhibit 1. Workers' attitudes toward productivity.

"In the organization or company where you work, what do you think would be the most effective way to encourage people to come up with good ideas to improve performance of the organization or company—would it be to promise a *money* reward, special *personal recognition*, or a *promotion* to a better job?"

Money reward	41%
Personal recognition	26%
Promotion	26%
Other	3%
No response	3%

"If you work hard in your job and do your best, do you think your supervisors or managers will notice this and give you a better job or not?"

Will notice; give better job	48%
Will notice, but not give a better job	23%
Will not notice, not give better job	23%
Don't know	7%

doesn't think he needs it, and (c) doesn't think it will do him any good if he gets it. What are your chances of making the sale?

According to most surveys, businessmen face roughly equivalent odds in their attempts to convince people that productivity improvements are in their interest. Although attitudes have improved somewhat in recent years, very significant numbers of employees still have only the foggiest notions of what productivity is all about. According to the Lou Harris/Sentry Insurance Survey of 1981,[14] less than one-third of workers think that productivity is "one of the two or three most serious problems facing the nation in the 1980s." When asked by the U.S.

Exhibit 1 continued

"If all the organizations and companies in the country improved their performance and productivity, who do you think would benefit the *most*—workers, management, stockholders, or consumers? Who would benefit the least—workers, management, stockholders, or consumers?"

	Workers	Management	Stockholders	Consumers	All of the above
Most	9%	15%	17%	39%	18%
Least	44%	12%	15%	13%	9%

"If you work hard in your job and do your best, do you think it makes a big difference in how *successful* your company or organization is, or don't you think it makes very much difference to your company or organization whether you work hard or not?

Makes a big difference	67%
Some difference	16%
Not very much difference	15%
Don't know	2%

Source: U.S. Chamber of Commerce
Survey Research & Productivity Center, 1981.

Chamber in 1981 to identify who would benefit most and least if productivity were improved, employees gave a fairly sophisticated answer: consumers would be the prime beneficiaries, they said. Regarding who would benefit least, employees pointed the finger at themselves. Only 9 percent of employees thought they'd benefit most if productivity were improved (see Exhibit 1).

Yet despite this basically negative picture of popular perceptions concerning efficiency, surveys also show that although workers don't understand productivity and don't think they'll benefit if productivity is improved, they still have ideas about how productivity can be enhanced.

Exhibit 2. Workers' attitudes toward improving productivity.

"Which two do you think it would be possible to change so as to bring about the largest improvement in performance and productivity in most companies?"

Workers' attitudes and abilities	53%
Management attitudes and abilities	37%
Supervisors' attitudes and abilities	21%
Quality of tools and equipment	21%
Amount of innovation and new technology	18%
Government rules and regulations	12%
Union practices	10%
Amount of investment in new plant and equipment	9%
Availability and use of computers	6%

Two fascinating readings, one from the U.S. Chamber Survey Research and Productivity Center (Exhibit 2) and the other from the Lou Harris/Sentry Survey (Exhibit 3), underline this point. In the first, employees were given a laundry list of ways productivity could be improved and asked to check off the two areas they thought would yield the best results. Though employees were given nine areas to pick from, more than half chose a single one: changing "workers' attitudes and abilities." An additional 37 percent thought the key was changing "management's attitudes and abilities." Are people trying to tell us something? In the second reading, conducted by Lou Harris/Sentry, employees were asked what actions their specific companies could take to encourage an overall productivity improvement. As before, employees were given a laundry list of things that could be done. In this case, they were asked to choose as many as they liked. The top choice, with a 43 percent

Exhibit 2 continued

"How much time have you spent thinking about changes that could be made in your company or organization that would improve its performance—a lot of time, some time, not very much time, or no time at all?"

A lot of time	44%
Some time	18%
Not very much time	31%
No time	7%

"If you had what you thought was a good idea that would improve the performance of your company or organization, how likely do you think it would be to be adopted—very likely, somewhat likely, not very likely, or no chance at all?"

Very likely	29%
Somewhat likely	36%
Not very likely	24%
Not at all likely; no chance	8%
Don't know	3%

Source: U.S. Chamber of Commerce
    Survey Research & Productivity Center, 1981.

selection, was (as might be expected), "employees getting financial rewards for productivity gains." In other words, "if you want productivity, pay us for it." The answers that tied for second place, with 42 percent, provoke more interest. They were "more and better information from management" and "employees being treated with more respect." Information and respect, in fact, which can't be pocketed, scored higher than job security, bonuses, better tools, better fringes,

Exhibit 3. Comparison of employees' and business executives' attitudes toward improving productivity.

Question: To what extent could overall productivity at your place of work be improved by (read each item)—a great deal, somewhat, only a little, or not at all? (Percentages represent those who say "a great deal.")

	Employees	Business executives
Employees getting financial rewards for productivity gains	43%	55%
More and better information from management about decisions that affect employees	42	40
Employees being treated with more respect by their supervisors	42	37
Better relations between management and labor	39	52
More favorable attitudes toward (your) employer	38	50
Employees having more say in decisions that affect them	37	16
Employees having a greater chance for recognition and promotion	37	40
Employees having more job security	36	11
Employees having bonuses which rise or fall depending on the company's profits	36	34
Having better fringe benefits	35	5
Use of better equipment and tools	29	67
Employees having less pressure on the job	26	3
Employees having safer working conditions	20	8
Having more pleasant physical surroundings at work	19	8
Employees having more convenient working hours	17	3

Source: Lou Harris/Sentry Insurance Poll "Perspectives on Productivity: A Global View," January 1981.

and safer working conditions, all tangibles that could materially change employees' lives for the better. If we want to motivate today's employee to improve efficiency, it's pretty clear that we cannot accomplish the task through material carrots alone.

BUSINESS: THE PUBLIC CASTS A JAUNDICED EYE

In *The Rhetoric*, Aristotle dealt with the question of how listeners evaluate a speaker. On the one hand, the listeners will judge the speaker by his or her words, logic, emotional content, delivery, and so on. On the other, the listeners will judge the words by how much credibility they put in the speaker. To Aristotle, the speaker's believability was his ethos. Thus, if you were to bring Richard Nixon in to talk on the importance of honesty in politics, most audiences would put little credence in his words. If Nixon, on the other hand, came to discuss the U.S.-China relationship, he'd probably get a respectful hearing. Nixon's ethos is such that his credibility on rectitude is low, while his expertise on foreign affairs is acknowledged.

In an era in which business is attempting to improve its communication efforts that target employees and the public, it's important that corporations understand how business is perceived; important because how we are perceived will often determine whether business will be believed.

The mid-sixties were a golden age for most Americans. As a whole, the nation reached new levels of prosperity while confidence in institutional leadership soared. Since that time, confidence in all major institutions has dropped precipitously. However, no institution has suffered a greater loss of regard than business. How bad do people feel about the corporate community?

- Public confidence in business was 66 percent in 1966. It fell to 13 percent by 1983.[15]
- According to prominent surveys, over 50 percent of the populace routinely accepts the pronouncements of Ralph Nader. Less than 10 percent believe corporate "op-ed" ads.[16]
- Only 10 percent of citizens in 1978 (*U.S. News*) said business

firms do a good job of providing "value for the money." In the same reading, 7 percent say business does a good job of "being honest about products."
- According to Yanklovich in 1979, over 50 percent believe that "big businessmen are generally immoral and unethical."

Happily, people have positive things to say about business as well. Business is admired for its work in promoting technological advances. People think that most employers try to pay fair wages. The public respects business's role in providing choices to consumers. Even so, none of this should obscure the fact that business is viewed by most of the public and most employees with jaundiced eyes. It is perceived by many as "greedy" and "self-interested." When business tries to communicate with employees, it must, if it truly wants to reach people, do nothing to reinforce these stereotypes.

THE WORKPLACE

Turn to any business magazine published over the past five years and flip through the pages. You won't have to search very far before finding a horror story on the problems of the contemporary American workplace. Whether the difficulties concern quality, absenteeism, labor/management strife, productivity, or satisfaction, we're in trouble and the problems appear to be getting worse. Moreover, it's becoming increasingly clear that many of these difficulties occur either as a reflection of employee attitudes, or could be improved by a change of outlook. Just what are people thinking about their jobs, their salaries, their supervision, and their role in the world of work?

Since 1969, the University of Michigan's Institute for Social Research has tracked employee attitudes for the Department of Labor. The results have been disheartening. Across the board, almost without regard to classification, people have grown more negative. In the job satisfaction section, for example, discontent increased between 1969 and 1977 in 21 out of the 22 areas surveyed. Whether the issue is benefits, salary, supervision, or opportunity, significant numbers of people are not happy.

This discontent spills over into the way employees perceive their employers and the products they make. According to a 1980 *L.A. Times* reading, 44 percent of employees think that the caliber of business management has gotten worse over the past 10 years, as opposed to only 16 percent of executives who agreed with that. According to a recent Gallup poll, 27 percent of employees say they would not buy the products they make. Taken together, these readings suggest that the *U.S. News* was conservative when it estimated in 1981 that a quarter of the workforce was discontent on the job.[17]

Yet, as is the case in so many other areas, employee ideas on what's happening on the job are paradoxical. While people are registering negatives on employment issues at a rate that rivals discontent during the Great Depression, their underlying commitment to the work ethic seems unimpaired. When workers were asked by the U.S. Chamber whether they felt that "it's important to work hard on your job and do your best," 88 percent said that it was (Exhibit 4). As a follow-up, when the same group was asked whether they'd "work harder and do a better job" if they were involved in making decisions that affect their job, 84 percent said they would. A recent Aspen Institute Study on the nature of work in the Western world rated the underlying work ethic of the American worker as second among the major industrialized states—behind the Israelis and ahead of the vaunted Japanese.[18]

Probably the most revealing conclusions reached from survey research on attitudes toward the workplace is the degree to which workers and managers agree on the extent of our contemporary problems. According to the Lou Harris/Sentry report previously cited, both groups feel, by margins generally in excess of 70 percent, that people on the job today don't work as hard as they used to, aren't as loyal to their employers, show less pride, do poorer work, and are not as motivated (Exhibit 5). People seem to be in agreement on the problems. The question is, how do you solve them?

THE ALIENATION FACTOR

When I was in college, I once asked a sociology professor which was the worst problem facing the country, "ignorance or apathy?"

Exhibit 4. Employees' commitment to the work ethic.

"What about how *you yourself* feel—do you think it is important to work hard on your job and do your best, or isn't it very important to you whether you do this or not?"

Important	88%
Somewhat important	8%
Not very	3%
Don't know	2%

"Of the things listed on this card, what would you say is most important to you about the job you have? What is second most important? What is least important?"

Most important	Second most important	Least important	
30%	14%	24%	Job security (knowing that I will not be laid off)
24	19	18	The satisfaction I get from my work
22	32	14	Money; salary
17	21	6	The quality of the work I do
5	12	34	Chance for a promotion to a better job
2	3	3	No response

"I don't know," he said, "and I don't care!"

For many years now polls have shown that by and large people lack any clear understanding of the economic system and the way business operates within it. In the larger society, people are often equally ignorant of who's representing them in Congress, how laws are passed, and how the world works. In recent years, however, it's become increasingly clear that large portions of the American population are becoming

Exhibit 4 continued

"Some people believe that if workers are involved and take part in making decisions that affect their jobs, they will work harder and do a better job. Other people believe it doesn't make very much difference. What do you think?"

Will work harder and do a better job	84%
Doesn't make very much difference	14%
Don't know	2%

Source: Ronald H. Clark and James H. Morris, "Workers Attitudes Toward Productivity," U.S. Chamber Survey & Productivity Center. Survey conducted by the Gallup organization, 1979.

turned off, both on themselves and on the possibility that they can effect positive change—in the workplace as well as in the large sphere of human action.

Jimmy Carter hit on this, perhaps our bottom-line problem, in a speech that turned out to be the most controversial of his ill-starred presidential career. On July 15, 1979, Carter came down from two weeks of contemplation in the Catoctin Mountain solitude of Camp David to give an address that may well have cost him a second term. In his speech, Carter blamed the problems besetting his presidency on a national spirit of "malaise" that made it impossible to rally popular trust and support behind his programs. There is, he declared, "a crisis of confidence that strikes at the very soul and spirit of our national will . . . The gap between our citizens and our government has never been greater."

Predictably, people blamed their lack of support on Carter's ineptitude rather than on their deficiencies. But, after all, was Carter right when he said there was a spirit of "malaise" throughout the nation? If so, does that attitude have any meaning for business executives as they approach the challenges of the eighties and nineties?

For every year since 1966, pollster Lou Harris has been testing people in cooperation with ABC News for what he calls "feelings of alienation." The results have been disquieting (see Exhibit 6). In 1966,

Exhibit 5. Perceptions of changes in the work ethic.

"Do you think most people today work harder or not as hard as they did 10 years ago?" (Percent responding "not as hard.")

Employees	63%
Business executives	62%
Total public	63%

"Do you think most people today have more pride in their work, or less pride in their work than they did 10 years ago?" (Percent responding "less pride.")

Employees	78%
Business executives	70%
Total public	76%

for example, 45 percent of the American people agreed with Karl Marx's dictum that "the rich get richer and the poor get poorer." By 1980, 76 percent agreed. In 1966, 37 percent of the people endorsed the view that what they thought didn't count very much. By 1980, 59 percent agreed. In what might be the saddest evidence of popular feelings of impotence, in 1966, 9 percent felt that they were "left out of things going on around them." In 1980, 41 percent agreed.

Why do people feel this way? Any number of reasons come to mind, from the effects of such events as Watergate, Vietnam, race riots and political assassinations, to the role of the media, to such sociological trends as the breakdown of the family, the decline of organized religion, and the transient nature of much of life in the late twentieth century. Perhaps it's simply "future shock," as Alvin Toffler put it. Whatever the cause, the effect strikes businesses in manifold and subtle ways. How can you effectively motivate those who are in essence detached and distrustful? How can you effectively compete with nations and competitors whose personnel, at least from outside appearances, are motivated and turned on?

Exhibit 5 continued

"Do you think employees are more loyal or less loyal to their employers than they were 10 years ago?" (Percent responding "less loyal.")

Employees	79%
Business executives	74%
Total public	76%

"Do you think that, in general, workmanship is better or worse than it was 10 years ago?" (Percent responding "workmanship worse.")

Employees	69%
Business executives	73%
Total public	71%

"Do you think that people's motivation to work today is stronger or not as strong as it was 10 years ago?" (Percent responding "not as strong.")

Employees	73%
Business executives	77%
Total public	73%

Source: Lou Harris/Sentry Insurance Poll "Perspectives on Productivity: A Global View," January 1981.

WHO IS TODAY'S EMPLOYEE?

"In hiring a worker," Peter Drucker wrote in 1954, "one always hires the whole man."[19]

Whether or not business has wanted to face it, whenever it enrolls a new employee, it enlists not just a worker's hands, but a person's heart and mind, and his or her ideas about the enterprise system, about

Exhibit 6. Feelings of alienation.

Question: Now, I want to read you some things some people have told us they have felt from time to time. Do you tend to feel or not feel that (read each item)?

	1966	1968	1969	1971	1972	1973	1974	1976	1977	1980
The rich get richer and the poor get poorer.	45%	54%	57%	62%	64%	76%	78%	74%	77%	76%
Most people with power try to take advantage of people like yourself.	x	x	x	33	39	55	58	56	60	64
What you think doesn't count very much anymore.	37	42	38	44	50	61	57	58	61	59
The people running the country don't really care what happens to you.	26	36	35	41	45	55	56	56	60	48
You're left out of things going on around you.	9	12	13	20	24	29	32	40	35	41
Index of alienation	29	36	36	40	44	55	56	57	59	58

Note: When more than one study was conducted in one year, the figures for that year have been averaged (1972, 1974, 1976). Index of alienation is average for all questions combined.

Source: The Harris Survey, ABC News. Latest survey December 11, 1980.

business, and about society.

Today's employee is, perhaps, more than the employee of other generations, a being who both participates in his or her world and critiques it. Collectively, many employees today don't like the view. On the negative side, they are critical of business and lack basic information on how the economic system works and what role they play in it. On the positive, they have confidence in the fundamentals of private enterprise and believe they are the key to our nation's economic renewal.

How, then, can business reach this disenchanted community?

4

The First Experiments

In February, 1975, Ray Shamie got mad.

A Massachusetts entrepreneur who'd risen from blue collar ranks to found a highly successful high-tech firm, Shamie had spent two decades building his Metal Bellows Corporation from scratch. Now, as he lifted his eyes from the grindstone for the first time in years, he contemplated the world around him. He didn't like a lot of what he saw.

The oil crisis was raging at that time, and corporations, which had already suffered a perceptible decline in confidence, were now really taking it on the chin, courtesy of OPEC and Watergate. "As I talked with people," says Shamie, "I found that they knew hardly anything at all about economics. People thought profits were 30, 40, 50 percent. They believed that businessmen were a bunch of greedy bastards, out to do you in. And I knew that that was wrong. My own experience in business had told me otherwise."

Like a lot of executives at that time (and subsequently), Shamie brooded about the lack of public understanding without knowing exactly what to do about it. Then he began to read extensively. "I became convinced," Shamie says, "that the problem was, if anything, worse than I'd thought. I wondered what kind of future business or private enterprise we could look forward to if large segments of the population didn't understand or accept the legitimacy of either."

METAL BELLOWS: AWARENESS PASSES MUSTER

Shamie decided to do something about his concerns. Calling up his local high school, he invited the principal to send 10 of his brightest students down to Shamie's plant for summer jobs combined with a course in business economics—which he intended to teach. Although Shamie soon found that the students knew even less about the market than their parents did, the sessions went well. So well, in fact, that Shamie got another idea. "If I'm doing this for these kids," Shamie thought, "why shouldn't I do it for my own employees? After all, their attitudes have an impact on my business."

That fall, Shamie called his middle managers together and outlined what was bugging him. Then he dropped the bombshell. "I told them I was going to close the plant down once a month to talk about private enterprise with everyone who wanted to discuss it. Moreover, I said I'd do it on company time. They didn't like it."

Shamie's people had two basic objections. First, they thought that the employees wouldn't appreciate it. They were convinced that people were indifferent to the issues Shamie cared about. Second, they contended that the program would be a significant productivity drain on the firm, an assessment Shamie agreed with. "Even so," Shamie says, "I thought it was important, so I decided to go ahead."

Over the course of the first year, Shamie found his employees undergoing a process similar to that reported by employee awareness coordinators in businesses across the nation.

At first, the employees were skeptical. Although they attended the sessions, probably because the boss was conducting them, it was plain that everyone was waiting for the other shoe to drop: that the point of it all was that they were going to get a pay cut or that the firm should stay nonunion. "At first," says welder Dino Pettiford, "I was sure the thing wouldn't go. Everyone was waiting around, saying 'What's this really all about?'"

When they realized that what the program really was all about—an attempt to explain both economics and the business they worked for—from the viewpoint of how it affected them—their interest was sparked. People started asking questions and looking for more information. Skepticism evolved into enthusiasm as Shamie's staff came to understand the stake they had in the corporation and the system. Finally, people got involved. The employees began running the awareness sessions (they still do today), sought means to improve the firm's efficiency, and became active in the community. Several employees ran for political office, and at least three won. Moreover, Shamie's employees, working on their own time, played a pivotal role in putting Massachusetts' Proposition 2½ on the ballot, a proposal that passed overwhelmingly and led to the single largest tax reduction in any state's history.

All of this pleased Shamie. But the executive had a further surprise in store for him. Corporate productivity didn't decline. Rather, it rose, and it rose dramatically. The profit picture improved too, while morale seemed to be significantly enhanced. "A program that was meant to be good for the country," Shamie reports, "turned out to be pretty good for Metal Bellows, too."

DART INDUSTRIES: TURNING AROUND NEGATIVITY

Just as Shamie was discovering that people had no love for business, Justin Dart, the colorful and controversial founder and chairman of Dart Industries, was reaching similar conclusions.

An executive who believed that "any CEO who doesn't spend one-third of his time in public affairs should be fired!" Dart was intensely interested in politics. His vision took him even further: corporations, he maintained, could not expect to be effective in pushing their legislative agenda if people were uninformed on economic issues and were generally hostile to business interests. Dart decided to do something about it.

Choosing for his experiment in economic awareness his West Bend subsidiary, a union plant located in Wisconsin, Dart had his local managers survey the company's 2,400 employees to find out how they felt about profits, productivity, their firm, and their own ability to effect change, both in the company and in society. The results confirmed what Dart had expected: people didn't know a heck of a lot. Less than 10 percent of the workers could even come close to identifying the amount of profit the firm made. Most thought the amount was between

25 and 40 percent. There was also a widespread consensus that the stockholders got to keep too much revenue and the employees got too little.

To see if they could begin to close this knowledge gap, Dart, West Bend president Bill Davis, and Ron Carson, the firm's communication director, developed a program. First, they sent a letter to every worker's home describing the program. Second, they used the corporate bulletin board as a medium to disseminate information. Rather than covering all subjects, the information focused on one topic each quarter. Third, they reinforced their efforts by handing out payroll stuffers on the same subjects and by running articles in the company newsletter. Finally, concurring with Dart's public affairs director Jim Lindberg, who predicted "if there's ever going to be an attitude change in any program, it would probably occur through face-to-face communication," Davis invited the employees to a series of meetings to talk with him on the topics.

Although all elements of the program were well received, the employee meetings turned out to be "particularly effective," according to Carson. After the test run, the survey was resubmitted. This time, 48 percent of the people got the profits figure right, an additional 20 percent were close, and there were substantial gains in overall knowledge in a variety of areas. A full 90 percent of employees wanted the program continued. As with Shamie's experiment, morale in the company seemed to improve markedly.

Satisfied with the results, Dart began a one-executive crusade to get other firms to follow his lead. Feeling that businesses that were trying to get involved would need some central authority to turn to for information and advice, he established the "Center for the Study of Private Enterprise" at the University of Southern California, under the direction of Arthur Laffer. During its four years of existence, it supplied "how to" information to hundreds of corporations.

SUNDSTRAND: ECONOMICS FOR EVERYONE

Shamie started his awareness program largely out of concern over the alarming direction private enterprise seemed to be taking. Dart was motivated by his involvement in politics. At Sundstrand, a large Illinois-based manufacturing firm, awareness got its start because of management's conviction that if people understood more about business they'd do their jobs better.

In truth, Sundstrand backed into its program. Reading the indicators that pointed to peoples' lack of knowledge about business, the manufacturer worked with a consultant to develop a supervisory training program on the subject.

Given its intended audience, The Sundstrand program was far more academic than the ones used at Dart and Metal Bellows. It featured five two-hour classes backed by a workbook. Even so, it differed from the "theoretical" approach to economic education in two regards. First, it emphasized how economic issues affect the individual. "Our philosophy," says Ron Harris, Sundstrand's manager of manufacturing operations, "was that most employees believe in free enterprise, but have a difficult time relating business success and profitability to *their* success and profitability." Second, Harris adds, "the key word was 'discuss,' not 'lecture.' " All of the sessions were taught by businessmen, not teachers.

After the first few sessions, the supervisors had become avid enthusiasts. They recommended opening the course to any of the rank and file "that would be interested." Expecting a modest response, management advertised the course to the firm's unionized workforce. Interest was little short of overwhelming; it was clear that Sundstrand had an unexpected success on its hands. Pulling back to regroup, Harris worked with managers at six of the firm's plants to make the program available to nearly everyone. In a little over two years, 4,500 employees, a third of the workforce, had taken the course. Pre-and post-testing of sample attendee audiences showed that their economic knowledge had increased an average of 30 percent.

"ECONOMICS OF SELF-INTEREST": OTHER FIRMS GET ON THE BANDWAGON

The proselytizing efforts of Dart and Shamie, the positive experience at such firms as Sundstrand and West Bend, and, more generally, the perception in business that a serious communication problem with employees and the public had emerged, prompted dozens of firms to enter the employee awareness field in the late seventies, with programs varying in quality and stressing different objectives.

At Coors in Colorado, the emphasis was on "saving free enterprise." Reflecting the conservative outlook of the Coors brothers, the brewer's elaborate program featured a weekly newsletter on economic issues, the usual collection of posters and payroll stuffers on economics, "Brown Bag Lunches" on a variety of issues, "Living Today" discussion groups for employees after hours, and a resource library for workers. The idea was to inspire people to experience what program director Fred Holden calls "the process": "aware, interested, informed, concerned, involved—in that order."

GTE, with nearly a quarter of a million employees, got into the act as well. Finding, according to special projects director George Royall, that few GTE employees "understood the role of profits, the causes of inflation, or the meaning of capital investment," the company developed what may have been the most ambitious employee awareness effort ever attempted. Convinced that most of the economic materials currently on the market were either propagandistic or too theoretical, GTE developed its own, all designed to be, in the words of public affairs director George Griffin, "economic education from the standpoint of the listener's self-interest." The materials included films, workbooks, passouts, and posters. Training sessions were run at corporate headquarters for presenters, who then fanned out to the corporation's multitude of facilities. Altogether, over 120,000 employees participated in group discussions on profits, inflation, and government spending in the first two years of the program. Reports from the field were positive, and follow-up survey results encouraging.

GTE addressed the problem of building employee awareness in a large corporation with a complex program. At Dana Corporation, Rene McPherson decided to handle matters more directly. Deciding that "nothing more effectively involves people, sustains credibility, or generates enthusiasm than face-to-face communications,"[20] McPherson determined that he'd go out and explain business and economics to all 40,000 of his employees personally. In over 200 sessions strung over three years, McPherson did just that. "In all my years of travel," he later observed, "I never got one cheap-shot question from an employee."[21] It is, of course, difficult to measure what sort of effect McPherson's visits had on the company. Even so, Dana quickly rose, under McPherson's leadership, from being a depressed and highly unionized "basic industry" to becoming one of the nation's most profitable corporations.

THE COMMON DENOMINATORS

As varied as the early economic awareness programs were, nearly all shared certain common features that made it possible for these firms to dismantle walls of apathy and distrust that had seemed unassailable before. Briefly, these elements were:

Meetings

People such as Dart and Shamie knew instinctively that simply providing employees with written information wasn't enough to change long-established attitudes. They realized that, at a gut level, today's employees often feel powerless and unheeded. They're barraged with ample one-way communications, courtesy of ABC, NBC, and CBS. By offering employees the opportunity to discuss issues of mutual concern on a regular basis with management in a nongrievance setting, corporate officials were sending out a subtle message: "We respect you, and think what you've got to say is important." This is precisely what employees want and need to hear. Because most of the programs ran on company time, everyone was reached; both the folks who normally get involved and the larger, more alienated masses, who generally don't.

Literature

Although the heart of the program was two-way communications, literature provided a backup for the points under discussion. Usually, the materials were simple and concise, without being simplistic. They ranged from some of the high-quality economics booklets that have been developed by the Ad Council, to *Reader's Digest* reprints (a generally excellent choice), to the ubiquitous payroll stuffers. Since the average person needs to hear something about 14 times before retaining it, the effective use of printed materials was an important supplement to the programs.

Topical Approach

Favored too was what Ron Carson at West Bend called the "total package concept." This involved picking one topic a month, quarter, or whatever, and tying everything—literature, meetings, activities—into that topic, instead of trying to explain the world to employees in a one-hour session. By spending a month on, say, profits, it was hoped that at the end of that time people would actually know something about the subject. It was further hoped that they'd be able to tie this lesson to the next topic.

General to Specific

Unfortunately, many managers have tenaciously stuck to the notion that employees are interested in their company's profit, not in the idea of profits per se. Thus, the theory goes, firms should leave the "free enterprise stuff" to the ideologues, and tell employees about the bottom line without bothering too much about communicating how that fits into the total welfare of society. Believing this, corporate officials are usually surprised when their own pronouncements to employees on their profit problems evoke yawns, or, in some cases, hostility. What went wrong?

Konosuke Matsushita, the founder of Matsushita, hit the nail on the head when he noted in his autobiography that "people need a way of linking their productive lives to society."[22] The fact of the matter is, today's employees don't care all that much about the profitability of their companies, provided they're not on the edge of collapse. They don't care because they don't know what profit is, don't see how it aids their long-term well-being, and don't see how it (and their contributions to it) advance the cause of their family or their society. Until workers ask the right questions and get the answers, they simply won't be motivated toward profitability, productivity, or other corporate goals.

By contrast, the early experimenters in employee awareness told people what profit was, *first*, and *then* told them about company profits.

"WII-FM"

Another commonality among the initiators of effective employee programs in the seventies was their awareness that most Americans are really tuned into station WII-FM: "What's In It For Me?" All their

> *Another commonality among the initiators of effective employee programs in the seventies was their awareness that most Americans are really tuned into station WII-FM: "What's In It For Me?" All their programs strove to answer that question for the worker, and in that sense, they were employee programs rather than corporate programs. Which is what they should be.*

programs strove to answer that question for the worker, and in that sense, they were employee programs rather than corporate programs. Which is what they should be.

Involvement

Perhaps the most effective message sent out by the early awareness programs was their gospel that the average individual could "make the difference"—in the workplace, in the community, and in the nation as a whole.

Bruno Bettelheim, the great Swiss psychologist, once pointed out that everyone has two basic and seemingly contradictory needs: "to feel part of the group, and to stand apart from the group and be recognized for one's own individuality."[23] Unless these needs were met, Bettleheim said, people could not be truly fulfilled or motivated. By holding awareness meetings, companies made people feel part of something: a firm, a society, an economic system. By providing opportunities for involvement, the programs gave employees a chance to "individualize" themselves. The antidote for alienation had been found.

TROUBLE SPOTS

Which was not to say that the initial employee awareness programs were problem-free. They decidedly weren't. Just as the early programs hit on many of the things that make employee awareness effective, they also ran up against some of the difficulties that can still make awareness a hit-and-miss operation.

Companies found three trouble spots:

Crusading

The 1940s awareness programs were sometimes accused of being propagandistic. The seventies programs, although far better than their predecessors, did not entirely avoid this scourge. At Coors, the initial awareness offerings provoked some resentment. The program was soon routed in a more centrist track. In California, Dart's "Private Enterprise Center" was asked to leave the USC campus after Dart's Reaganite sympathies became too visible.

Leadership change

Although highly popular with employees and clearly effective, West Bend's program was all but terminated after Bill Davis's departure for another firm and Justin Dart's death last year. The GTE program, also widely admired, suffered a similar fate.

Lack of Supervisory Support

As anyone involved in the "quality circles" movement will attest, the biggest stumbling block to building effective employee participation programs is middle management resistance. Awareness offerings are not exempt from this rule. At Metal Bellows, Ray Shamie started his program against the wishes of many of his managers. To this day, 10 years later, attendance at the voluntary sessions among the rank and file is almost universal, while supervisory participation remains spotty.

THE LESSONS LEARNED

Despite these difficulties, the experiences of the seventies showed that "employee awareness" was once more a viable concept. The nay-sayers who had insisted that employees would not like such programs had been proved wrong. Those who'd contended that union resistance would present an insurmountable obstacle were refuted by the examples of excellent programs in such union firms as Sundstrand and West Bend. Moreover, it was clear from the surveys run by many of the better experimenters that "employee awareness" programs, when run correctly, could indeed achieve the desired goals of changing attitudes and improving knowledge.

Yet the most exciting results of the early experiments were the ones that had been largely unlooked for and unexpected. The programs had not only benefited the workplace educationally, they'd also provided, in many cases, psychological and material boons as well. Communications and morale had been boosted, productivity problems seemed to diminish, "community" had started to replace "confrontation," and people had gotten involved.

Modern employee awareness was born.

5

Modern Employee Awareness

"Nothing so focuses the mind," Mark Twain once wrote, "as the prospect of being hung."

As the nation lurched into the economic crisis of the late 1970s and early 1980s, lots of minds in corporations, unions, and the public sector were forced to focus on what had made this country great in the first place—and on what had gone wrong. Through this process of introspection, long-established precepts were challenged, revered ways of doing business were cast aside, and a new relationship between our central economic actors—business, labor, and government—emerged.

Just how great is the change? Turn on the radio for a day or two and listen. You'll hear the damndest people saying the damndest things. Union leaders are calling for more loyalty to employers, liberal congressmen are describing businessmen as "economic heroes," corporate officials are admitting that managerial incompetence has had as much to do with declining productivity as "big government." These changes are by no means universal. In fact, the majority of businessmen, labor leaders, and politicians are still tracked in their familiar grooves. Even so, this should not obscure the tremendous transformations that are taking place in contemporary corporate management.

It's Their Business, Too—47

One of the clearest trends is the movement toward more participation in companies by employees. There's hardly a major firm in the nation today that's not involved in one form of "participative management" or another, from "quality circles" and "quality of work life" programs, to ESOPs and building worker input into such things as job design, goal setting, and charitable contributions by the company.

By the same token, employee awareness programs have emerged from their 1970s half-life to become again, as they were in the fifties, a significant part of the corporate scene. In the past two years, new programs have been developed at two of General Motor's new auto plants, at John Hancock, Dennison, Reader's Digest, Huffy Corporation, Norton, Hallmark, and in dozens of other firms. In the small business field, the National Federation of Independent businesses (NFIB) has launched a major project designed to assist its 500,000 members in establishing "awareness" programs. Throughout the nation, managers are being invited to "how to" seminars designed to teach program development skills. Clearly, employee economic awareness is an idea whose time has returned. The question is, why?

ORIENTAL PERSUASION

Much of the impetus for the expansion of "awareness" programs in recent years has come from Japan.

With the Japanese model, Americans were confronted with ways of organizing work that differed sharply from those typical of firms in this country. Whereas we manage by giving orders, Japanese firms rule by "consensus." Whereas working Americans tend to believe that "a job's a job" (nothing to get excited about), their counterparts in Japan are expected to regard the company as "family" and to immerse themselves in the affairs of their firm. While American executives believed that quality came from strict inspection, the Japanese knew that quality came from individual employees who were determined to produce it, backed by a management determined to get it. As Japanese productivity improvement rates skyrocketed in the seventies (while ours stayed flat), and as our docks groaned with the weight of imported Japanese steel, autos, cameras, and electronic gear (while American factories sat learn, and that management is the appropriate teacher.

However true, these word choices simply won't wash with today's employee. Workers today are better educated than their parents were, distrustful of authority, and deeply suspicious of "established wisdom." One-third of all living Americans were born during the "baby boom," and, as a popular saying from the sixties went, "You can't tell them anything." A lower but increasingly significant portion of the workforce was born in the post-baby-boom sixties. While as a group these folks

> ***"Awareness" is a better and more accurate term for what an employee program should be, suggesting as it does a general raising of consciousness and cognitive powers. This is a process very much in line with today's various movements toward "self-fulfillment."***

are less rebellious than their older brothers and sisters, they're also more cynical. Both of these constituencies will quickly "turn off" on anything that sounds like a lecture.

"Awareness" is a better and more accurate term for what an employee program should be, suggesting as it does a general raising of consciousness and cognitive powers. This is a process very much in line with today's various movements toward "self-fulfillment."

Permissive—Not Dogmatic

The implicit assumption behind the previous programs was that "management knows best." Although questions would certainly be entertained, it was clear to program sponsors and attendees alike that the bosses had all the answers, or thought they did.

Today's employee already knows that management isn't always right. They've seen pictures of Youngstown and are far more up-to-date on such issues as "greenmail," toxic waste, and Japanese quality than management suspects. Programs that extend a vision of managerial infallibility insult employees' intelligence. Worse, they're counterproductive, in that they tend to stifle the impulse of many to share their student." "IBM," the piece continued, "was aligned with the world situation in the employees' minds."[30] Justin Dart and Fred Clark would have been glad of that.

THE NEW PROGRAMS

Just as the impact of the Japanese experience and the publication of *In Search of Excellence* and similar works encouraged companies to try employee awareness, they also significantly influenced the nature of the programs. In a matter of a few years, employee awareness changed from a course in "economic understanding" to something far more inclusive. Today's "employee awareness" programs bear almost no resemblance to the offerings of the 1950s. At the same time, they're markedly different in substance and structure from the programs of the seventies. Employee awareness has grown up.

Understanding the differences between "awareness" offerings present and past is important if we wish to gauge the suitability of "awareness" to meet many of the communication needs of the contemporary corporation. Taken together, the distinctions are both subtle and profound.

In many basic areas, there are few differences between today's programs and those Justin Dart offered at West Bend in the mid-seventies. Employee programs still center around meetings, still feature an emphasis on discussion, still try to explain to the employees "what's in it for them." Wise firms who've gotten involved in recent years have favored the topical approach and taken the time to relate the issues they've discussed to the realities of the external world.

The divergences are largely a matter of emphasis and nuance. Six areas prominently outline the differences.

Awareness—Not Education

The programs of the fifties were billed as "economic education." Some were and some weren't. Justin Dart and Ray Shamie referred to their offerings as "employee information." The terminology in both cases is based on the assumption that employees have something to

EXCELLENT ATTITUDES

Similarly, the publication of Tom Peters' and Bob Waterman's *In Search of Excellence* also inspired the move to "employee awareness."

Declaring as their goal the study of what makes American companies "excellent," Peters and Waterman spent three years visiting some of the nation's most prominent firms, evaluating the keys to their success. Many of the "keys" turned out to be themes traditionally emphasized by employee awareness advocates.

Declaring that, in the words of Peters, "excellence is a matter of attitude,"[26] the pair advised companies to pay special attention to "the care, feeding, and unshackling of the average man."[27] Excellent companies, they found, went out of their way to provide information to employees about the business and about how the company related to the outside world. Approvingly they quoted management expert Anthony Athos to the effect that "good managers make meanings for people as well as money."[28]

Conveying to employees the idea that they were respected was regarded as vital, too. For Peters and Waterman, productivity improvements were seen not as the result of incentives given to top executives, but rather as gains stemming from the "extraordinary efforts of ordinary people." "Was there any link between productivity and communication?" Peters was recently asked in a published interview. "Absolutely!" he declared, "One hundred percent! On every dimension! . . . Any activity that brings people together or serves as a channel for information is worth doing. Look for any excuse to get people together to communicate."[29]

Possibly the sweetest vindication of employee awareness in *In Search of Excellence* came in the form of Peters' and Waterman's defense of that executive rarely defended in corporate circles: the crusader. Declaring that every major firm in America had been created, in Peter Drucker's memorable phrase, by "a monomaniac with a mission," the pair advocated that modern executives and employees get enthusiastic, engage in creative hoopla, have fun, and believe passionately in what they're doing. Citing the case of IBM, Peters and Waterman uncovered a 1940 *Fortune* article which described Tom Watson as having "the appearance and behavior of a somewhat puzzled divinity idle), many reached the conclusion that the Japanese were, perhaps, doing something right.

This realization prompted the movement toward "employee awareness." The reason is obvious; much of what Japanese companies do to explain corporate goals to workers strongly resembles what "awareness" programs have been designed to achieve.

As with American "awareness" efforts, Japanese communication programs try to send employees two important messages. First, recognizing that man is, as Plato defined him, "a being in search of meaning," they show how the work that the company does has value for the whole of the society. Second, they tell the individual employees that, by working cooperatively with their peers, they can "make a difference," both for themselves and for others. Whereas in America, traditional corporate programs explain profits, productivity, and the like from the viewpoint of what's good for the shareholders (if they bother to explain them at all), in Japan, says Peter Drucker, "the group is expected to fit what serves self-interest into a framework of national need, national goals, national aspirations and values."[24]

Japanese management literature is replete with similar pronouncements. As William Ouchi pointed out in *Theory Z*, "In Japan the chief executive officer will typically write a book describing his own personal interpretation of the company's philosophy. Included will be an explanation of how the company and its employees can best serve the company and the nation through their productive efforts."[25] Typically, in Japanese companies, the "big picture" is communicated constantly. Company songs reinforce basic concepts; publications talk about the economics of the business; executives start the day at factories with pep talks concerning the firm and how it fits into the current world situation. At Matsushita, employees are asked to speak extemporaneously every few months concerning the firm's values. Altogether, it amounts to an oriental version of "employee awareness."

Which is not to suggest that it deserves to be emulated. Much of Japanese "employee awareness" bears a striking resemblance to the American programs of the fifties, at least in terms of their sloganeering and conformistic attributes. Despite this, the fact that "awareness" programs were prevalent in Japan, and were clearly getting results, certainly encouraged American executives to see if they could develop better programs of their own.

It's Their Business, Too—49

insights about what's wrong with the company, the economic system, or the way management runs things. Good programs are based on the presumption that management will learn as much from workers as workers will learn from them. Programs are "permissive" in that they frankly acknowledge mistakes and solicit "feedback," both positive and negative.

Universal—Not Externalized

The employee programs of the "eagles"—people like Dart and the Coors brothers—were almost wholly externalized. They talked about our productivity, capital investment, and profitability problems largely from the national perspective. Clearly, the "message" ran, these difficulties were manufactured in Washington, and would have to be solved there.

By contrast, the "ostriches," the typical corporate communicators, speak of economic problems only when and as they affect the company—if they speak of them at all. The PR journalist's ability to bury disaster in rosy semantics is legendary. One imagines a corporate newsletter announcing a nuclear war with the headlines, "D.C. Plant Closes for Repairs" and "Canned Food and Bible Publishing Divisions Report Record Sales," followed by 50 pages of "We regret the passing of. . . ."

These approaches are flawed. What happens in the firm impacts the employee, as does what happens in Congress. Both deserve coverage. Ideally, employee awareness programs should give employees at least a taste of what Peter Drucker has called "the managerial vision": that sophisticated understanding of the factors, internal and external, that contribute to corporate and, hence, personal success.

Integrated—Not Singular

The traditional employee information program was just that: a program. And, in some cases, it met the fate of all too many "corporate programs"; it was heralded with trumpets and banners, flourished briefly, and then succumbed slowly to the combined pressures of work schedules, production crunches, and waning managerial enthusiasm.

By contrast, today's "awareness" program is designed to be integrated into the way the company does business. Whereas in the past there was a clear distinction between "The Program" and "The Business" (guess who loses over the long run?), managers of contemporary offerings make no such distinctions. At Huffy Bicycles, for example, industrial relations director George Plottner sees the awareness program as helping to satisfy a number of corporate objectives, one being to stimulate more involvement in the firm's quality circles program. Quality circles director Mike Hazley sees the sessions as one way of letting his circles people know just how important productivity is to everyone. At its optimum level, an employee awareness program should serve as a sort of "central nervous system," sending signals regarding goals, issues, projects, and opportunities for involvement throughout the corporate body.

Participatory—Not Hierarchical

Just as past employee programs assumed effective managerial omnipotence, so too they presumed that all the natural leaders in their firms wore ties. They were wrong on both counts.

Men like Justin Dart strongly felt that an employee program would fail without the direct and visible support of the CEO. In this, they were surely right. They also believed that, to the extent possible, top management should attend the programs. This was wise, too. When top management attends awareness sessions, it sends out a signal to both the employee and the supervisor that "this is important."

Where Dart and company went wrong was in assuming, one, that top management would continue to focus its interest on the program month after month, year after year; and, two, that employees would continuously regard as an "employee program" something that was clearly another managerial tool, however well-intended.

Metal Bellows' Shamie was the first to see this. About a year after starting his program, he turned its direction over to a "steering committee" of rank-and-file employees, who've been running the program ever since. "They've done more with it," admits Shamie, "than I'd ever have had the time or the imagination to do."

In Worcester, Massachusetts, the awareness program at Wright Line, Inc., is similarly directed. The current committee chairman, machinist Greg Vasale, got the post after he put up a hand during a session on productivity and told the corporate president that the new machine he was pridefully describing was "a piece of junk." Looking into the matter, the president concluded that the machinist might have a point. Vasale's thinking was just the sort he wanted to encourage, and the president invited him to help direct the employee program.

If the purpose of awareness programs is, in part, "to unshackle the average man," if the idea is to "individualize" people and show them what they can do, then there's no better way to get this "message" across than by involving employees in planning and conducting it.

Holistic—Rather than Targeted

One of the symmetries between the employee programs of the fifties and those of the seventies is that both were "targeted." They considered business and economics and precious little else. Because of the rationalist assumptions that underlined these programs, they were designed to avoid questions concerning the operations of their specific firm, the way moral values interacted with the issues, the impact of change on personal lives, and such other extraneous matters. After all, they didn't want to get people confused.

What the early program directors forgot is that, as Peters and Waterman put it in *In Search of Excellence*, "the central problem with the rationalist view . . . is that people are not very rational.[31] Just because the "ground rules" say awareness programs only concern economics, this doesn't mean that the employee is going to think only about economics or ask only about economics. The pioneers also neglected to deal with the fact that, as Buckminster Fuller posited, "man is a comprehensiveness." People not only want to understand economics; they also want to know about politics, about their communities, about personal computers, the space program, and how to write their wills. Further, they want to understand the relationships among these things.

Modern employee awareness programs try to meet these needs by being holistic. While ensuring that a core of information is provided on vital topics, they also see to it that general worker interests are addressed. The goal is both practical and psychological. Recognizing that we live in a highly integrated world, the people directing today's employee programs realize that a session on "saving your heart" could produce benefits in reduced health care costs, while one on "how to write your legislator" could also have its future uses. Further, many companies now see that the basic reason so many people are resentful toward business and other forms of institutional leadership is that they feel powerless and isolated in their own lives. To the extent that firms can, through awareness, help employees sort out, comprehend, and effectively manage a complex, confusing, and sometimes frightening world, alienation and distrust can be replaced with confidence and cooperation.

WAKE UP! AMERICA!

"Compared to what we ought to be," said the philosopher William James, "we are only half-awake. We are making use of only a small part of our physical and mental resources."

When Ray Shamie started his awareness program in 1975, he christened it with a typical "eagle" name: "Wake Up! America!" What Shamie probably wanted people to wake up to was the need to "save free enterprise" from Ralph Nader and the advocates of "big government."

On the surface, Shamie's title articulated a certain naivité about the complexities of the world and about what was considered appropriate in correct corporate circles. In a deeper sense, however, Shamie had hit the nail square on the head. The phrase "Wake up, America" has a powerful simplicity.

In essence, the purpose of employee awareness is to "wake up America," not just to the need to "save free enterprise," although that's part of it, but also to the dangers and opportunities posed by a rapidly changing world. Moreover, the goal is to "wake up Americans" to the fullness of their own resources, as individuals, as a team, as part of the freest and most productive society the world has ever known.

If this goal could be fully accomplished, there's probably little that the successful company could not achieve, either in terms of motivating employees or enhancing their productivity. The question is, how do you get started?

6

Getting Started

"That which is well-begun," said the poet Horace, "is half-concluded."

For most firms that become involved in employee awareness, that which is done or not done in the first few months in large part determines how successful the program will be. To the extent that management can effectively articulate the need for the program to middle managers and union representatives and to the degree that it can excite the interest of the rank and file and encourage their participation, the program will meet with rapid acceptance and begin producing results. To the extent that management fails in these tasks, program progress will be slowed or arrested entirely. Bad first impressions are the ones most difficult to correct.

In order to get off to a good start, managers should, before initiating awareness sessions, ask themselves the same series of questions that journalists pose before writing a story.

WHY? GOALS AND OBJECTIVES

The first question management should ask itself is "why do we want to do this?"

In all too many cases, awareness offerings have gotten their start more as an expression of executive *angst* than out of any serious contemplation of how such programs could serve corporate and individual needs. Typically, a CEO would hear a speaker at a Chamber breakfast (me, perhaps), rail about the way business and free enterprise were being maligned. Incensed, the executive would rush back to his office, determined to "do something." A year or so and many dislocations later, the boss would take a second look at what he'd wrought. Not knowing what exactly it was that he'd wanted to accomplish, the official was damned if he knew whether he'd achieved it. Having had no idea of where the program was supposed to go, he'd usually be at a loss to determine whether he'd gotten there. Depending on how much money, ego, and real enthusiasm had been invested in the offering, the program would then be shelved, overhauled, or allowed, in the colorful words of the immortal John Erlichman, to "twist slowly, slowly in the wind."

These difficulties can easily be side-stepped if the program is properly planned and its objectives are communicated before it's introduced. As a first step, management must determine what its basic motivation is in initiating the program. Just what are you trying to achieve?

Keep in mind that motivations vary, for the simple reason that firms vary. At Reader's Digest, Bob Jockers, the program's initiator, "wanted to help people understand free enterprise." At General Motor's new auto plant in Wentzville, Missouri, the idea "is to get everyone on the same wavelength" concerning such issues as quality, teamwork, and the competitive challenge. John Hancock, operating in the heavily regulated insurance industry, wants, according to legislative director Barbara Burgess, "to get everybody thinking about how the political process works," while at Hallmark the goal is expressed in a way that leaves little doubt as to why the card maker is regarded as one of the best firms to work for. "It just seemed to us," says training director Roy Benner, "that it was the right thing to do."

Increasingly, companies have been opting for holistic rather than targeted programs for the reasons outlined in Chapter 5. Whatever your company's motivations, they should be stated and understood up front. Moreover, it's generally a good idea to write them out and discuss them. Such a "statement of awareness program purpose" can serve, later on, as a good tool for evaluating program success. It will also help you determine if you've changed your own outlook on what's important as a result of the sessions.

WHO? THE PROGRAM COORDINATOR

Regardless of who ends up carrying the awareness ball in any given company, he or she will be forever subject to the one immutable rule of the game: unless they have the full backing of top management in the play, they're going to fumble. In employee awareness, management support must be stated, it must be visible, and it must assert itself when, as occasionally happens, the going gets rough. Dart Industries' Lindberg put it very bluntly: "Without the support of the CEO, you're dead."

The history of management support of employee programs has had something of a checkered career. Most of the early programs were actually started by executives. Unfortunately, some of them also were washed up when the executive left the firm, lost interest, or died. In other businesses, managers have assigned staff to run employee programs, and directed their attention elsewhere, with compromised results. When, as is happening more frequently, employees have been asked to run the offerings, executives have sometimes assumed that the problem of direction has been solved, and that their further involvement would "inhibit" the nonexempts. Wrong. It's precisely when the rank and file is running an awareness program that management support, sans interference, is most vital.

By the same token, no one in top management should allow the requirement of "personal support" to scare them off a program. Although it's quite possible for an executive to spend a good deal of time in this area if he wishes, the time commitment required to demonstrate backing in most sizable companies is modest. What's called for is attending most meetings, doing an occasional presentation as the need arises, providing recognition and rewards to those doing the work, and communicating frequently to middle managers your interest in the program and enthusiasm for the achievement of its goals. In most situations, this will "get the message" across to everyone.

When top management understands and accepts what will be required of it, it's time to give consideration to who, on a day-to-day basis, will run the program. There are three possibilities:

The CEO

In some of the early awareness programs, the CEO took direct responsibility for running the awareness sessions. This has certain advantages. First, the chief executive knows the business and how the outside world affects it. Second, such direct intervention on the part of the boss certainly gets the idea across that the program has backing from the top.

For smaller firms, direct CEO management is an option that can be seriously considered. In larger firms, it's simply not practical. Then again, a recent study concerning how Japanese executives behave may call into question just what usages of executive time *do* get results. Convinced that the secret of the success of Japanese firms must rest, at least in part, on how Japanese CEOs manage their time, a research team spent a year following prominent oriental leaders around. They expected that the Nipponese execs would spend their waking hours plotting strategies and planning export drives. Instead, they found them attending employee weddings, giving out awards, and otherwise devoting themselves to ceremonies and people problems. Is there a lesson here?

Staff

Most firms will assign their employee awareness responsibility to someone on staff. When companies do so, they should keep in mind that employee awareness isn't just another job—and it can't be looked on as just that by a program coordinator who wants results. Bluntly put, this means that the right person has to be as sold on the concept personally as top management is. Moreover, he must have the ability to project his enthusiasm onto others.

Any organization of more than a few dozen employees will have people who fit this bill, if it looks for them. To be honest, they often aren't found in personnel departments, where people are frequently trained to manage misery rather than find creative ways to prevent problems. The type of person the company might look to would be the employee who is also a town councilman, the executive who's active in Junior Achievement, the lady who used to run her own business. Whoever is selected, the choice has to be made with care. Employees will often judge the program by their perceptions concerning the character, competence, and commitment of the person presenting it.

Bringing in a Consultant

A third option concerns hiring a consultant to run the awareness program. This approach has both pluses and minuses.

On the positive side, you'll often get a more polished program than you can put forward on your own. Also, a good consultant who's had experience in the field can help you dodge some of the mine fields that await the naive awareness entrant. In some cases, someone from "outside" will have more credibility with employees than management does.

On the negative, unless he's particularly skilled, a consultant can come off as too polished, which is a "turn off" to the rank and file. Worse, since the consultant is not an employee of the business, he will know less about it, and this will show.

As a general rule, the consultant option should be appraised on a case-by-case basis, with staff people preferred when good choices are available, and "experts" selected when inner resources are lacking or the distrust level is particularly high.

WHAT? PROGRAM DESIGN

As soon as a program coordinator is selected, he or she will have to determine what sort of program should be offered. Given the "objectives" that have already been established, what configuration of meetings will lead to the desired result?

In making these decisions, the program director, in consultation with top management, has to make several determinations that will have a critical effect on what sort of awareness sessions he or she will be running. Among the issues for consideration are:

Frequency

How often should programs be held? Monthly? Bi-monthly? Quarterly? It should be kept in mind that the more space you put between programs, the less collective impact they'll have.

Company Time?

Should employees attend on company time? Or should the program be offered "after hours"?

Both formats have been used successfully, but strong preference should be given to "company time" programs. The reason is simple. To the extent that employees have to make an effort to attend, those employees who really *need* to be involved (the alienated ones) won't be there; the ones you're already reaching probably will be.

Running awareness programs on company time isn't always easy. It frequently requires that programs be offered in multiple sessions, sometimes at odd hours. However, when the will to accomplish the task is there, a way around these difficulties can usually be found.

Internal or External?

Another issue that needs to be resolved is whether the program presenters will be drawn from outside the company, or whether they'll be developed internally.

Small to medium-sized firms usually prefer outsiders. This makes good sense. First, internally, in corporations of less than 1,000 employees, there aren't likely to be a large store of acceptable presenters. Secondly, outside speakers, if well selected, can bring a unique and varied perspective.

For very large companies, bringing in "externals" may not be a practical option, except on special occasions. In these circumstances, the coordinator will have to determine who will present the materials, how they'll be trained, and so on. Large firms such as GTE, Hallmark, and General Motors have had ample experiences in these areas, and can be called on to share information.

Formats

Once topics have been selected, the coordinator has to determine what program formats will be used to present them. In most firms, information is generally offered through lectures, even though this is the most "high risk" presentational style. There are, in fact, at least four options to choose from: lectures, lecture/film combos, panels, and debates. Using all four from time to time will inject variety into the program.

Employee Involvement

Just how far are you willing to go? Is the objective simply to provide some understanding? Or do you want to utilize your program, in part, to give people a chance for more participation in your firm?

As a general rule, employees will play this game by the rules you set up. They'll accept the awareness program as a lecture series on economics or as a total change in your corporate culture, depending on the signals you send. Whatever those signals are, you should be prepared to follow through on whatever you're implicitly promising.

On all these issues, and on the choice of topics for presentation as well, the program coordinator should solicit opinions and advice from people in management, from union officials, and from knowledgeable employees. While not promising to include any specific subjects or concepts, the coordinator should synthesize this input into positive ideas that can aid in developing the proposed plan. Even before the coordinator presents the plan formally to middle management, he or she should have a pretty fair idea about the direction the sessions will take.

During the first year, selection of topics should be generally structured around the so-called "Three I's", which are:

Insights. Surveys have repeatedly shown that employees lack information on the basics of economics, business, and politics. Insight programs are designed to provide this information and should serve as the essential building blocks of any awareness program. An "insight" session on profits, for example, would discuss what profits are and how profitability relates to the individual's welfare.

Issues. Issues programs place individual industries and communities within the framework of the basic information offered in the insight programs. Continuing the profit example, a follow-up program might consider the profitability of your particular industry, and what factors influence it.

Involvement. Any awareness program that attempts to tell employees what's wrong with the country, their industry, or their company, and then offers them no means of correcting these problems, will do nothing but add to the depression of people who are alienated enough. Every program should offer realistic suggestions on how employees can influence the issues under discussion, whether that involves telling them how they can volunteer to join quality circles, reduce their intake of fats, write their congressmen, or whatever. The more advanced a program becomes, the more often such "involvement" oriented sessions should be the focus of the effort. An "involvement" "profit" session would stress what the employee could do to enhance corporate profitability.

The Fourth "I": Interest. In addition to including the "Three I's" in his or her program plans, the coordinator should also consider the "Fourth I," which is, by far, the most important.

That's interest.

Awareness programs can be factual and informative, but if they're boring they won't have the desired impact. You can invite an acknowledged expert to your plant to lecture on an important topic, but if your audience doesn't see how that topic relates to their personal situation, you won't reach them.

How can employee programs be kept interesting? First, by making sure that all issues are addressed in such a way as to relate them to your attendees' needs, problems, and pocketbooks. You must hit the employee where he lives! Second, favor speakers with a down-to-earth style rather than someone projecting an academic air. Third, and most important, good programs regularly solicit employees for their ideas. Topics that employees suggest are generally the ones most relevant to their interests.

Combining all these concepts, the program coordinator should be able to develop a series of awareness programs that will provide useful information to employees in an entertaining way while inspiring involvement, improving communications, and meeting corporate goals. When the program coordinator feels that the program has reached this point, the time has come to present it to middle management.

WHERE AND WHEN? THE MANAGEMENT MEETING

At a recent meeting of employees involved in managing awareness programs in the Northeast, a survey was sent around the table. Part of the poll asked the question "What has been the single factor that's most inhibited the success of the awareness program in your company?"

Of those who responded, 80 percent said "supervisory resistance." In introducing an employee program, there is no factor so crucial to long-term success as getting supervisors on the program's side early and enthusiastically. How do you do it?

When the program coordinator has fully developed the awareness plan, he or she should seek its endorsement by top management. That accomplished, both the program and the plan should be formally introduced to the middle management team and, where appropriate, to the union bargaining unit.

At the introductory session, the CEO should express his support for the awareness concept, and should:

- Explain why the company has decided to become involved; identify goals;
- Comment on why awareness is important to the company, to its employees, supervisors, and union;
- Briefly introduce the program; and
- Solicit opinions and advice.

The coordinator should speak next. He should review:

- Details of the program;
- Materials to be used;
- The experiences of others in the awareness field; and
- The role of management in promoting the program's success.

Frank discussion should be encouraged. The management meeting can be extremely useful, not only in winning support for the program, but also in giving the coordinator important insights into what sorts of special problems the program might encounter and how the sessions could best be managed to maximize their impact.

Once the program has been sold to top management and communicated to leaders at the supervisory and union levels, it should be introduced to the rank and file.

INFORMING EMPLOYEES

Before initiating the awareness sessions, the chief executive officer should send all employees a letter announcing the program. The letter should be brief, personalized where appropriate, and informative. It should solicit comments and suggestions concerning the program as the sessions progress.

Where possible, the introductory letter should be sent to the employees at home. There's a better chance that it will be read. Further, by sending it home, you will introduce the employee's family to the concept. This is important, since the reaction of the employee's family to the awareness program will, in part, shape the employee's own outlook.

At this time, management should also decide whether it wishes to use a survey to measure program effectiveness. On the plus side, a survey can aid in tracking how effective a program has been in improving knowledge and attitudes. On the negative, a survey also implies to the employee that he's being tested to see if he has the "right" ideas. If a survey is to be used (a sample is included in Appendix A), it should be sent with the introductory letter, and resubmitted after a year. A 20 percent return should be considered statistically accurate.

By following the guidelines listed in this chapter, you will have laid a solid foundation for an effective awareness program. You will have established rational goals, developed a firm plan of action, sold it to supervisors and union officials, and introduced the concept to the folks that all this activity has been directed toward, the employees.

After all this work, you'll be anxious to conduct your first awareness sessions, which is as it should be. That, after all, is where the fun comes in.

7

Managing Awareness

During its initial year, an employee awareness program should attempt to accomplish four objectives. First, it should seek to *overcome skepticism*; second, it must engage workers' *interest*; third, it should generate real *enthusiasm*; and finally, it should begin the process of *employee involvement*.

THE FIRST MEETING

What happens at the first employee session will go a long way toward determining how rapidly these goals will be achieved. If the meeting is successful, employees will quickly perceive that your program benefits them, and will support it. Fall short of conveying this message, and progress will slow.

Several things have to happen if the initial awareness session is to have maximum impact. Primary among these is the necessity of making the support of top management manifest, either by having the first sessions "kick off" with a brief introduction by the CEO, or by having a suitable message from him read by a high ranking official. Next in importance is that someone, either the chief executive or the program coordinator, outline the company's reasons for initiating the sessions. That person should emphasize that "awareness" is an employee program, and that management seeks and would appreciate comments and suggestions concerning what's being offered. Finally, the first and all subsequent sessions should be designed to encourage discussion. It's only when employees start talking that a program really becomes "two-way" communication.

As early as the opening session, the learning process should start—for both parties. Just as the audience will make a judgment concerning the presenter, the program coordinator should start to analyze his or her audience. Among the things to note are expressions of employee likes and dislikes; evidences of their individual strengths and weakness; and statements that reflect general attitudes. All this information should be used to fine-tune the programs and help guide the coordinator to those employees who could, in the future, contribute the most to assisting and directing the meetings.

In terms of style, there are errors that presenters will want to side-step. First, they should avoid talking too much! They should let the employees carry the ball, at least for part of the time. Next, during the discussion period, coordinators should shun telegraphing the "right" answers. Presenters must be "permissive," entertaining all viewpoints and doing nothing verbally or in terms of body language to express disapproval. Talking over employees' heads, or, worse, being condescending, will kill a program before it gets started. When communicating with employees, keep in mind "Sturgeon's Law," first articulated by a prominent science fiction writer who used this philosophy in writing "Star Trek" scripts: "never overestimate their information and never underestimate their intelligence."

Whoever runs the program should always keep in mind that the way they conduct themselves will do more to "sell" the awareness concept to workers than anything any single speaker can say or do. Whenever managing sessions, the program coordinator should be positive, specific, honest, and enthusiastic, without overselling. The coordinator should, at the close of the first and every meeting, make sure that employees know what will happen next. In that way, people will soon see the "links" between issues, so vital to building any real process of understanding.

Hopefully, the initial program will reach a standard of quality that will allay suspicions and excite interest. How do you keep the ball rolling?

UP AND RUNNING

Four elements influence the ability of awareness programs to keep the attention of their audiences over months and years. These are variety, creativity, relevancy, and consistency.

Variety is important to avoid the "tomato soup syndrome," the habit of feeding people a constant diet of nutritious but bland awareness offerings. To some extent, variety in programs can be enhanced by utilizing different program formats. If you've had a series of lectures, for example, try a debate. Or bring in a film or a panel. In a larger sense, variety is best promoted by covering an array of different topics in intriguing ways.

Being creative will accomplish this. Instead of getting an economist, have your program on profit conducted by a well-known local entrepreneur. Replace your productivity specialist at a session on a newly purchased machine with a guy from the floor who's learned to operate the thing. Virtually any potential topic can be given an innovative "twist" that will enhance interest.

Throughout this process, though, bear in mind that what really gets employees to respond to awareness is relevancy and consistency. If workers feel that the topics you're addressing relate to their needs, they'll respond. If they see, by means of the "linkages" between the issues you present, that the program is going somewhere, they'll stick around until you get there.

The longer a company runs awareness programs, the more it becomes apparent that the sessions fit into four rough "categories," as follows:

Economic awareness. Sessions in this area should be the basic building blocks of any program, for all the reasons covered in Chapter 3. Potential topics include profits, productivity, private enterprise, and interest rates.

Company-related. Discussions of your competitive situation, product lines, quality programs, and communication problems fall in this category. All this is important, but these topics should not be allowed to dominate if you expect people to regard "awareness" as an "employee" rather than a "company" program.

Public and community affairs. Particularly popular in heavily regulated industries, such sessions cover local and political issues on a nonpartisan basis. If handled properly, these programs can effectively convey to employees the idea that the firm "cares" about society's welfare. Remember the 1940 report about IBM "being aligned with the world situation is employees' minds."?

Employee service. These sessions cover a compendium of programs designed to assist the employee in his or her personal life. Popular topics include financial planning, personal health, substance abuse problems, and handling stress. Employees are attracted to these programs, for obvious reasons. Kept in proper proportion, they serve management by helping the employees feel in control of their own lives. This, in turn, reduces alienation and enhances trust.

Most corporations will put stress on some topics more than others. This is entirely appropriate, since the needs of firms vary. Wise companies, however, will include meetings drawn from each of the groups. Such "holistic" programs do a much better job than "targeted" offerings that attempt to reach and fulfill the needs of everyone.

RESOURCES

Newcomers to employee awareness usually view with dread the prospect of finding resources to run their programs with. Where will they locate the literature, films, and speakers they'll need?

Such fears are largely unfounded. One of the advantages of the 40-year history of employee awareness is that there's a vast array of resources available that have been created for use in employee programs. Further, a number of organizations exist to help you locate them. (See Appendix B).

Still, some general guidelines apply to the sorts of resources a coordinator should favor. We'll review a few.

Literature. Literature should be used to *support* a program; it should not *be* the program. Ideally, materials should be timely, concise, and written in everyday language without being condescending. Program directors should try to provide literature from a variety of sources and from different points of view.

Reader's Digest is an excellent source of passouts. It makes reprints of many of its best articles available at attractive rates, and its pieces are written at a reading level that will be comfortable for just about all employees.

Films. These can be used both as programs, in combination with speakers, or to supplement programs. However, be careful in your choices! Many of the films created by business groups and corporations are truly dreadful—biased, condescending, and poorly produced. A notable exception is *Forbes* magazine's "Some Call It Greed."

The best films often derive from such TV shows as ABC's "20/20," CBS's "60 Minutes," and, especially, PBS's "Enterprise." Prints and tapes are available at reasonable rates.

Speakers. Next to developing a sound plan and picking a good coordinator, a program's success rests chiefly on the selection of speakers. Anyone with the responsibility of directing awareness offerings should give careful thought to what sorts of presenters he wants and whether they're to be drawn internally or externally.

The two most important ways to guarantee that a speaker will be effective are to (a) preview him, and (b) know your audience. If you have a fair understanding of your employees' needs and preferences, you'll also have a good idea of how well a speaker will go over.

Some general watchwords:

- Be wary of academics. All too often, they're used to "captive audiences," and won't work to reach employees.
- Favor speakers with "street smarts." People who deal with the public (police, salesmen, and so on) are often good choices.
- Employees, unlike many of their employers, prefer speakers who are direct, and they hate someone who "beats around the bush."
- Theory and statistics put people to sleep. Anecdotes and humor usually work.

In actuality, speakers are easy to find. Local chambers of commerce, trade groups, and service organizations can lead you to a variety of possibilities.

PARTICIPATION: UNLOCKING POTENTIAL

"Democracy," Jefferson wrote, "is based upon the conviction that there are extraordinary possibilities in ordinary people."

In a like manner, employee programs are premised on the belief that informed and involved workers can make significant contributions to their companies and their communities. If awareness is anything, it is a key designed to unlock underutilized and sometimes, sadly, unrecognized human potentials.

Some companies engaged in awareness stop short of encouraging involvement. This is somewhat akin to putting a key in a lock and refusing to turn it. Why is participation important?

> **Employee programs are premised on the belief that informed and involved workers can make significant contributions to their companies and their communities. If awareness is anything, it is a key designed to unlock underutilized and sometimes, sadly, unrecognized human potentials.**

First, it enhances credibility. People will truly believe your employee program is just that when employees are running it.

Second, participation improves communication. Even the best program director can only guess at workers' needs when designing meetings without employee input. Involvement can assure that awareness sessions reach their maximum level of effectiveness.

Third, involvement encourages problem solving, in both the program and the firm.

Fourth, activism fights alienation. People who are involved seldom feel isolated.

Fifth, participation builds worker self-confidence. This, in turn, provides motivation.

Sixth, involvement stimulates enthusiasm. When employees get enthused about the job, about the company, or the system, they become "monomaniacs with missions." To the degree that happens, the overall quality of their performance improves.

If a company wants to get full value from its investment in an employee program, it should utilize awareness as a tool to stimulate participation.

THREE PHASES OF INVOLVEMENT

Employee participation in awareness programs generally takes place in three phases. Ideally, a company will, over a period of a year or two, bring its people along step by step, from relatively low degrees of involvement on to the more advanced forms.

At the simplest level, employee participation can include asking employees by means of surveys to evaluate programs and make recommendations, as well as involving employees as presenters in areas where they have special expertise. Even awareness offerings with more modest goals should make provisions for this kind of participation.

The moderate level of involvement is occupied by the "steering committee." Ever since Ray Shamie introduced the concept at Metal Bellows in 1976, "steering committees" have proliferated. Probably half of the long-established awareness programs in American corporations today are run by such groups today.

At base, a "steering committee" is a band of rank-and-file employees selected by management to manage awareness programs. In the typical firm, management will, through a coordinator, run the program for about a year in order to give people a "sense" of what awareness is all about. Gradually, the reins will be turned over to employees, who will select the programs, locate speakers, preview materials, and collect input regarding the sessions from their peers.

Finding "steering committee" members is seldom difficult. The obvious candidates usually make themselves known to management well before the time has come to select the panel. As a rule, the "steering committees" membership ought to reflect the sorts of people who work for the company, both in terms of jobs and demographics. As individuals, committee members should have a positive outlook, be broadminded, and respected by their peers.

In recent years, some companies have moved toward more sophisticated methods of participation.

The central aspect of advanced "awareness" programs is the use of program sessions as a sort of corporate "central nervous system." In this model, information is communicated up from various levels of the business—productivity, sales, company community, and public affairs

—and disseminated throughout the corporate body by means of the meetings. Where helpful, involvement is sought through the sessions, as structured by the steering committee. Employees are asked to help form quality circles, are involved in registering their fellows to vote, assist in communicating information about profit-sharing results to each other, and are solicited to support activities as the United Way and Junior Achievement. Employees communicate through the program both the results of their work and the need for progress in other areas. In this sort of advanced employee awareness framework, the only constriction to the degree of involvement and the positive results that can be achieved will lie within the boundaries of the creativity of all the participants.

In other words, the potential is nearly limitless.

8

Afterword: The Greatest Revolution

Nearly one hundred and forty years ago, the great but now largely forgotten French free-market economist, Frederick Bastiat, wrote the phrase he said summed up his philosophy. "All legitimate interests," he declared, "are in harmony."[32]

Ironically, the same year the dying Bastiat wrote these words, two unknown intellectuals in Brussels were working feverishly on a document that would reach other conclusions entirely. In their *Communist Manifesto*, Marx and Engels portrayed a world in turmoil, divided by history into "classes" whose interests were forever inimicable. Ever since, these two viewpoints have framed most economic debate and have largely shaped the world we inhabit.

At the time all three were writing, 1848, Europe had entered the first phase of the Industrial Revolution. Through the deployment of machinery, productivity soared to levels unheard of in human history. Living standards climbed as well, at least for many. But as the role of machinery grew, the impact of individuals on their immediate world appeared to shrink. The seeds of alienation had been sown.

Some 50 years later, the industrial world moved into its second period of paradigmatic change. Through the efforts of Frederick Taylor and Henry Ford, the processes of work became standardized. Scientifically organized routine replaced chaotic and inefficient methodologies. Once again, the innovations brought about dramatic improvements in prosperity and efficiency. There was a cost, however, expressed perhaps most passionately in Charlie Chaplin's "Modern Times," a film that angered many because it cut too close to the bone.

In today's world, we are perceiving the outlines of the Third Industrial Revolution. If we peer closely, we can catch glimpses of it in the movement toward quality circles, in the trend toward an "information society," even in the highly individualistic faces of those Cabbage Patch Kids, so different from Barbie and Ken.

> **In today's world, we are perceiving the outlines of the Third Industrial Revolution. If we peer closely, we can catch glimpses of it in the movement toward quality circles, in the trend toward an "information society," even in the highly individualistic faces of those Cabbage Patch Kids, so different from Barbie and Ken.**

As the transition occurs, there will be no clear demarcation lines. Whereas the previous transitions were marked by changes in methods, this one will be gauged by changes in minds. While the previous changes standardized, the next one will individualize. Although the last alterations emphasized the machines of man, the next one will focus on realizing the potential of the greatest machine ever known: man himself. Altogether, the effect will be not to alienate but to liberate, not to promote conflict, but to help make manifest the truth spoken by Bastiat so many years ago.

"The greatest revolution," William James wrote, "is the discovery that human beings, by changing the inner attitudes of their minds can change the outer aspects of their lives."

The greatest revolution is happening now. Employee awareness has a role to play in it.

Appendix A

SAMPLE EMPLOYEE SURVEY

Introductory letter:

Dear Employee:

Before starting our employee awareness program, we would like to get your views on some of today's economic problems. This will assist us in preparing a better program.

Please answer as many questions as possible. Also, please feel free to comment on the program. Do not sign the survey. All answers will be kept confidential.

Thanks for your help!

PART A

Listed below are a number of statements. We would like to know how much you agree or disagree with each statement. Please check the appropriate box for *each* statement.

	Agree Strongly	Agree	Unde- cided	Dis- agree	Strongly Disagree
1. One of the most important causes of inflation is that business makes too much profit.............					
2. Over the years, as factories install more efficient machinery, there are more and more jobs for people............					
3. The typical big company is really above the law; it can get away with just about anything.............					
4. Economic progress in the United States is explained largely by the free enterprise system which we have.......					
5. Manufacturing firms are more concerned about how their products are advertised and sold than how they are made.............					
6. Automation may have helped businesses increase profits but has seriously hurt most American workers.............					
7. The government should take over and operate unprofitable companies rather than let them close down and put people out of work.............					

8. In general, business will not do any more to control environmental problems than is ordered by law ....

9. Money invested in new machinery and equipment has benefited the owners of the business more than the workers. ....

10. Except for public utilities, the best means of setting prices is to let buyers and sellers seek their own interests in a market free from government interference and control. ....

11. Most companies exaggerate or twist the facts in their advertising and do not really tell the truth ....

12. On the whole, big business no longer discriminates against minorities in hiring and advancements ....

13. In a situation where our natural resources are in short supply, the government—instead of business—should determine how these resources will be used ....

14. The country would be better off if the government put a tight lid on the percentage of profit any business can make. ....

15. The ability of companies to earn profits is essential for the survival of the American economic system ....

16. The working man is better off under the American economic system, considering its overall strengths and weaknesses, then he is in any other country ....

17. In the long run, profits are the best measure of how well a business serves its customer's needs ....

	Agree Strongly	Agree	Undecided	Disagree	Strongly Disagree
18. Most companies charge fair prices for their products.	___	___	___	___	___
19. Most companies in the United States can afford to raise wages 10% without raising prices.	___	___	___	___	___
20. My company is a good place to work.	___	___	___	___	___
21. Most big companies have grown big because they use their economic power to control the market.	___	___	___	___	___
22. The men who run the country's biggest companies really cannot be trusted.	___	___	___	___	___
23. The average person's voice doesn't count for much in forming government policies.	___	___	___	___	___
24. Somehow, the American economic system does not work for me.	___	___	___	___	___

PART B

Below are statements which you might hear on any particular day. Please give me your evaluation of how true they are. Check one box for *each* statement.

	Almost Always True	Usually True	Unde- cided	Usually False	Almost Always False
1. "One of the problems businesses face today is finding enough capital so that they can expand and grow"	___	___	___	___	___
2. "A good way to curb inflation is for the government to reduce unemployment"	___	___	___	___	___
3. "Our standard of living is higher than in other countries because our level of productivity is higher"	___	___	___	___	___
4. "Of the total money taken in by manufacturing companies, more goes to the stockholders in dividends than to the workers in wages and salaries"	___	___	___	___	___
5. "One of the causes of our inflation is that people are being laid off"	___	___	___	___	___
6. "Workers in the U.S. earn more than in other countries because the equipment and machinery they use allows them to produce more than workers in other countries"	___	___	___	___	___
7. "The surest way to raise the country's standard of living in the long run is to limit profits and increase wages"	___	___	___	___	___

	Agree Strongly	Agree	Undecided	Disagree	Strongly Disagree
8. "The main function of competition is to prevent large firms from driving small ones out of business"					
9. "Government control over corporate profits would lead to fewer new and improved products for consumers"					
10. "An unprofitable company is usually a poor place to work"					
11. "The most likely result of increased investment in machinery and equipment for a company would be an increase in cost of products to consumers"					
12. "Competition is wasteful because it means too many companies are making the same thing"					

PART C

We would also like your views on employee information programs.

1. Business should share more information with their employees concerning:

    a. Company policies   ( ) Agree   ( ) Disagree

    b. The company's role in the marketplace   ( ) Agree   ( ) Disagree

    c. Community problems   ( ) Agree   ( ) Disagree

    d. National problems   ( ) Agree   ( ) Disagree

    e. Economic issues related to the company's welfare   ( ) Agree   ( ) Disagree

2. If my company decided to run meetings concerning economic issues on company time and on a voluntary basis, I would ( ); would not ( ) want to attend them.

3. I would like to see employee information programs on the following issues (check two):

( ) Energy ( ) Inflation ( ) Productivity
( ) Health Care ( ) Profits ( ) Elections/Politics
( ) Regulations ( ) Nuclear Power ( ) Jobs
( ) Social Security ( ) Taxation ( ) Other _____

4. Provided that I found the initial meetings of the employee information program interesting and worthwhile, I might ( ), or probably wound not ( ) be interested in joining with other employees in evaluating and planning future meetings.

We would appreciate any comments you might have concerning the employee information programs.

_____
_____
_____
_____
_____
_____
_____
_____

Appendix B

RESOURCES

The following persons and organizations provide assistance in establishing employee awareness and related programs.

American Productivity Center
123 North Post Oak Lane
Houston, Texas 77024

Dr. William Petersen
Center for Economic Education
University of Tennessee
  at Chattanooga
Chattanooga, Tennessee 37402

Robert Moxley
Chamber of Commerce
  of the United States
1615 H Street N.W.
Washington, D.C. 20062

Sally Graves
Free Enterprise Institute
Amway Corporation
Ada, Michigan 49355

Betsy Schwammberger
National Federation
  of Independent Business
150 West 20th Avenue
San Mateo, California 94403

Brenda Bronson
Productivity Communication
  Center
6 Beacon Street, Suite 1110
Boston, Massachusetts 02322

It's Their Business, Too—85

Footnotes

1. See Lipset, S. M., and W. Schneider. *The Confidence Gap.* New York: Free Press, 1983.
2. *The Practice of Management.* New York: Harper and Brothers, 1954.
3. Clark, Fred G. *Economic Illiteracy and National Disunity.* New York: American Economic Foundation, 1946.
4. Ibid.
5. *The Affluent Society.* Boston: Houghton Mifflin, 1958.
6. *The American Challenge.* New York: Antheneum, 1979.
7. See Harrison, B., and B. Bluestone. *The Deindustrialization of America.* New York: Basic, 1982.
8. *Working.* New York: Pantheon, 1972.
9. Ibid.
10. Ibid.
11. Quoted in *Newsweek*, November 8, 1980.
12. Mayo, Elton, quoted by Peters, T. J., and R. H. Waterman, Jr., in *In Search of Excellence.* New York: Harper and Row, 1983.
13. Ibid.
14. Harris, Lou. "Perspectives on Productivity: A Global View." Stevens Point, Wisconsin: Sentry Insurance, 1981.
15. See Lipset, S.M., and W. Schneider. *The Confidence Gap.* New York: Free Press, 1983.
16. Ibid.
17. See *U.S. News,* April 6, 1981.
18. See the Aspen Institute, *Work and Human Values: An International Survey of Jobs in the 1980s.* New York: Aspen Institute, 1983.
19. *The Practice of Management.* New York: Harper and Brothers, 1954.
20. McPherson, Rene, quoted by Peters, T. J., and R. H. Waterman, Jr., in *In Search of Excellence.* New York: Harper and Row, 1983.
21. Ibid.

22. Matsushita, Konosuke, quoted by Pascale, R. T., and A. G. Athos in *The Art of Japanese Management*. New York: Simon and Schuster, 1982.
23. Bettelheim, Bruno, quoted by Peters, T. J., and R. H. Waterman, Jr., in *In Search of Excellence*. New York: Harper and Row, 1983.
24. *Toward the Next Economics*. New York: Harper and Row, 1981.
25. *Theory Z*. Reading, Massachusetts: Addison-Wesley, 1982.
26. See "Discoveries in Search of Excellence." Exxon USA, Second Quarter Report, 1984.
27. *In Search of Excellence*. New York: Harper and Row, 1983.
28. Quoted by Peters, T. J., and R. H. Waterman, Jr., in *In Search of Excellence*. New York: Harper and Row, 1983.
29. See "Discoveries in Search of Excellence." Exxon USA, Second Quarter Report, 1984.
30. Quoted by Peters, T. J., and R. H. Waterman, Jr., in *In Search of Excellence*. New York: Harper and Row, 1983.
31. Ibid.
32. Bastiat, Frederick, *Economic Harmonies*. Irvington-on-Hudson, New York: Foundation for Economic Education, 1964.